PORTFOLIO TEACHING

A Guide for Instructors

Nedra Reynolds

University of Rhode Island

Bedford/St. Martin's   BOSTON ♦ NEW YORK

FOR BEDFORD/ST. MARTIN'S

Developmental Editor: John Sullivan
Production Editor: Arthur Johnson
Production Supervisor: Donna Peterson
Marketing Manager: Karen Melton
Editorial Assistant: Katherine Gilbert
Copyeditor: Barbara Sutton
Cover Design: Donna Lee Dennison
Composition: Annika Tamura
Printing and Binding: Malloy Lithographing, Inc.

President: Charles H. Christensen
Editorial Director: Joan E. Feinberg
Director of Editing, Design, and Production: Marcia Cohen
Managing Editor: Elizabeth M. Schaaf

Library of Congress Catalog Card Number: 99–65249

Manufactured in the United States of America.

5   4   3   2
f   e   d   c

For information, write: Bedford/St. Martin's, 75 Arlington Street, Boston, MA 02116
(617-399-4000)

ISBN: 0–312–19809–4

Preface

Portfolio Teaching: A Guide for Instructors invites writing instructors to put portfolios at the center of their classroom practices and encourages them to keep their own teaching portfolios. I present some of the benefits of portfolios for teaching writing, rhetoric, and self-reflection. In chapters that review planning the course, responding to writing, and grading the portfolio, I try to alert teachers to potential problems or contradictions and help them to find the portfolio practices that best suit their own preferences, student needs, and program requirements. My intended audience includes veteran teachers who have yet to try portfolios, experienced teachers who have tried them but discovered problems, new teachers who want ideas and guidance, and writing program administrators who would like to recommend a textbook on portfolios for their teaching assistants and adjunct faculty.

Because writing portfolios have almost infinite variations — flexibility being one of their strengths — it would be very difficult to cover, or even anticipate, every possible form that writing portfolios might take; thus, my emphasis is on teacher-graded classroom portfolios. After reviewing the multiple ways that portfolios can have a central role in a writing class, I emphasize those particular approaches that I have found most useful or appropriate for my classes. While I don't dwell on the vast literature available on portfolio assessment, much of this literature has influenced my teaching and my presentation here, and interested readers will find an annotated bibliography on portfolios at the end of this volume, along with another bibliography of teaching resources.

With a focus on reflection and responsible choices, *Portfolio Teaching* works as a companion volume to (but not necessarily as an instructor's manual for) *Portfolio Keeping: A Guide for Students*. The latter is intended to be a supplemental or ancillary text for first-year college composition courses that rely on process pedagogy and emphasize rhetorical strategies and critical thinking. While the student volume follows, roughly, the sequence of a process writing course, *Portfolio Teaching* helps teachers make decisions before the course begins or when considering changes to their current course designs.

Teachers using *Portfolio Keeping* in their writing classes will want to assign its two major sections in two parts — early in the course and as the course begins to wind down. *Portfolio Keeping* first prepares students for what they can expect from a portfolio-centered writing course and then guides them in making connections among what they are learning about the writing process, rhetorical choices, and the situation of the portfolio.

I wrote both books because, despite the popularity of portfolios and their uses in elementary and secondary classrooms, portfolio keeping is still a new idea for many of my students (at a fairly large state university in the northeast). Most of them arrive in the first- and third-year courses I regularly teach without having kept a writing portfolio before. I wrote *Portfolio Keeping* for them, and *Portfolio Teaching* for all of the busy teaching assistants, overworked adjuncts, and overcommitted faculty who don't believe that they have time for portfolios.

Acknowledgments

I would like to thank Patrick Bizzaro of East Carolina University and Bill Lamb of Johnson County College for their helpful criticisms and advice on a draft of the manuscript. Chuck Christensen and Joan Feinberg at Bedford/ St. Martin's made this book possible, and John Sullivan made it happen. I am grateful for their collective ideas and insights. Katherine Gilbert helped gather books and reviews. Arthur Johnson guided the manuscript through production, and Barbara Sutton expertly copyedited the manuscript.

Contents

— INTRODUCTION —

Portfolios as Classroom Companion

After just one semester of using portfolios in my composition classes, in the fall of 1991, I could no longer imagine teaching without them. Portfolios are not "the answer" to teaching writing well; nor are they free of flaws or problems. They are, however, an important companion to process pedagogy and to rhetoric-centered writing classes, and they have energized my teaching. Portfolios balance an emphasis on the writing process with a strong emphasis on the final product and on the rhetorical decisions that inform that product. With the portfolio method, students have more reasons to revise, and I find more ways to be surprised.

At the same time, I'm well aware of the so-called grading burden of portfolios and of other difficulties with integrating them, and this volume addresses both the benefits and the challenges. Many teachers find portfolios too time-consuming or too unwieldy. Instructors attracted to portfolios are often put off by a vision of grading not one final paper for each student at the hectic end of a term but three or four or five papers. One of my goals in this guide is to encourage those interested teachers who have hesitated to try portfolio pedagogy by providing some concrete strategies for planning and orchestrating a portfolio course, from integrating reflection to grading the final portfolios.

The case I want to make in *Portfolio Teaching* is that portfolios give writers more time to develop and give teachers more room to provide formative evaluation. Portfolios provide a context for evaluation or assessment and focus the writing class on such skills as organizing and presenting materials, making informed and responsible choices, and reflecting on learning and course content. For these reasons and others, writing teachers at many levels have found portfolios rewarding, in ways I hope my readers will discover for themselves.

Portfolios have become hugely popular and influential in education, and they have supporters in several different camps. Classroom teachers like portfolios because portfolios are flexible and encourage reflective and responsible learning. Students like portfolios because they invite creativity and allow for choices. Educational theorists like portfolios because they support student-centered learning and critical thinking. Testing specialists like portfolios to test writing, at least when compared with multiple-choice grammar and usage tests or one-shot timed essay exams, but they are still debating about portfolios as a reliable assessment method for large-scale testing.

1

Experts do agree that writing portfolios measure what they are designed to measure — that is, portfolios give a better sense than most assessment designs about writers' ideas and choices; about their confidence, style, or felicity with language; and about their ability to make rhetorically sound choices and present work to a discerning audience. Researchers and teachers also seem to agree that portfolios support learning above and beyond testing situations and are a welcome asset to writing classrooms at all levels.

PART ONE

BACKGROUND AND BASICS

—1—
Defining Writing Portfolios

The National Council of Teachers of English supports the use of writing portfolios. The following statements appeared in *The Council Chronicle* (June 1997). While some particulars of this list may be more suited to elementary or secondary classrooms, the principles hold true for college-level classes.

Our Beliefs about Portfolios

- Improving learning and teaching is at the heart of the portfolio process.
- Contents and format are negotiated between student and teacher. The portfolio can take a variety of forms; there is no one right way.
- Student choice is essential. The students must select and reflect upon the contents within the negotiated parameters.
- Purpose and audience determine what goes in the portfolio and how the portfolio is organized and shared.
- Reflection is an essential element; without reflection, the portfolio is merely a collection.
- The creator of the portfolio talks about it with a variety of audiences. The portfolio is never handed to someone without its creator present.
- The portfolio process is woven into daily classroom life; it is not saved for the end of the month or trimester.
- The portfolio process is most successful when teachers first create their own portfolios and share their own process and portfolio with students and other audiences.
- The portfolio process celebrates student accomplishments by thoughtfully describing the learner.

Like most good ideas, portfolios aren't really "new." As Peter Elbow and Pat Belanoff relate, once portfolios had become very popular several years ago, veteran teachers, especially at the elementary level, began to speak up about their own "portfolio" methods (1997, 22). Long before 1986, when the Belanoff and Elbow program at the State University of New York at Stony Brook attracted so much national attention, portfolios had been familiar in art and investing. Artists keep some of their best works in a portable case or folder, ready to display the pieces that represent their interests, potential, or changes over time and to show to teachers, gallery owners, employers, or a jury of other artists. Financial managers keep records of stocks, bonds, mutual funds, or other investments to review periodically and to update as needed. Similarly, teachers or faculty members compile "portfolios" in the form of tenure packets or promotion files or annual review reports. In these versions and many others, the portfolio is not static but changes according to recent achievements, expanded ideas, or new interests.

A writing portfolio, then, is a collection that represents the writer's best work. Collected over time and across projects or interests, a portfolio showcases a writer's talent and hard work and demonstrates the ability to make thoughtful choices about content and presentation. It is a final product meant to be shared with others — perhaps to be evaluated or just to be enjoyed by friends or family. A teaching portfolio collects a variety of documents related to a teaching life: assignments and reflections on how they worked, course designs or curricular units, pages from a teaching journal, samples of responses to student writing, materials for an in-service day, thank-you notes from former students. Teachers keep portfolios to track their way through a new course, new school, or new curriculum; or to show evidence of teaching excellence to supervisors or future employers; or, perhaps most important, to practice reflective teaching, to model portfolio keeping for students, or to understand portfolios from a different perspective.

DIFFERENT TYPES OF PORTFOLIOS

Portfolios for educational purposes are usually of two broad types — learning portfolios and assessment portfolios — and they share the principles of choice, reflection, and variety. What follows is a review of the two types of portfolios and the key principles that inform portfolio keeping.

Portfolios for Learning

Some approaches to portfolios are specifically for the benefit of students, with or without some evaluation of their work. If learners are asked to keep a learning portfolio, they are invited to keep, collect, and create a portfolio for their own benefit, not to prove to teachers, or coaches, or supervisors that they should pass a course, receive an award, or get a promotion. Learning portfolios invite students to collect or create a variety of artifacts — essays, photographs, charts, letters, and so on — that best represent their experiences and engagement with the learning process in a particular subject area. Sometimes learning portfolios are revised to become a presentation or evaluation portfolio.

Portfolios for Presentation or Evaluation

A presentation or evaluation portfolio also promotes and sustains learning, but it shifts the attention, at a certain point, from the learning process to a final product. These types of portfolios vary widely, but they share a similar goal: to show someone else what the portfolio keeper has learned, or to convince an audience of the portfolio keeper's achievements, abilities, or talents. An artist puts together a portfolio to show to gallery owners or employers, or a writing major designs a portfolio to show to editors or graduate program directors. Similarly, students in a variety of courses keep portfolios to show the instructor, at semester's end, what they have learned from the course and applied to their portfolio's contents.

Whether a learning or assessment portfolio, the following three major principles define writing portfolios for most situations: choice, reflection, and variety.

- **Choice** Portfolios are designed, ideally, to give writers room to choose what to include and how to arrange and present the entries. If portfolio keepers are "told" what to include, where to include it, and in what form, there will not be nearly as much learning in the process. Keepers of *learning* portfolios make dozens of choices. Keepers of *assessment* portfolios also make many choices, often different ones. While writers make choices, selections, or decisions at every stage of the writing process — some of them unconscious or hardly recognized — the portfolio method allows some of those choices to be more conscious. No matter what type of portfolio is involved, good decisions are important to the reflective process and the final product. Helping students to manage and inform those choices is one of the jobs of portfolio teachers.

- **Reflection** Portfolios let writers look at their writing in a different way, taking into account several years, months, or weeks of work rather than just one assignment or task. Sometimes called *reflective learning* or *self-assessment*, this part of the portfolio method asks writers to take a careful look at their own patterns, strengths, and preferences for negotiating writing tasks, for learning a new skill, or for practicing a complex set of skills like those required for reading and writing. Almost every form of the portfolio method of assessment asks portfolio keepers to go a step beyond putting the portfolio together: They need to be able to articulate *why* certain choices were made or what those choices are meant to convey. Educational theorists use the word *meta-cognition* to describe the ability of people to think about their own thinking. *Meta* means "after," "behind," or "beyond," and *cognition* means the act or process of knowing. Thus, meta-cognition is the ability to "know beyond one's knowing," or to think about one's own thinking, usually after an assignment or task has been completed.

- **Variety** Because writers have different strengths and different interests, portfolios try to celebrate and cultivate these differences. A writing portfolio invites students to show off their writing abilities across different kinds of assignments, for different audiences, or with a different amount of time spent on each entry. *Variety* means more than different genres or types of writing; it also includes pieces of different lengths, written for different purposes, at different points in a writer's life — even if just at Weeks 2 and 12 in a college semester. A portfolio's variety is one of the reasons that it is considered a more "valid" measurement of a person's writing ability, especially when compared with a timed, multiple-choice test on grammar, usage, punctuation, and mechanics. Portfolios for school assessment include more than one sample and pieces written at different times, giving teachers or evaluators a fuller picture of someone's writing abilities.

Within these principles of choice, reflection, and variety, writing portfolios can have several differences. What follows are some common variations on the portfolio method for writing classes; you'll want to consider which of these variations fits best with your course goals or your writing program.

- **A writing folder** Students are asked to submit all drafts, notes, outlines, scribbles, doodles, and messy pages, representing all of their writing, finished or unfinished. Everything is saved, if only for simple record keeping, but students may also be asked to select from the folder two or three of their most promising pieces to revise for a "presentation" portfolio (see p. 8). For example, John asks his students in a first-year composition class to bring their writing folders to each class. To check that students are keeping their papers organized and labeled, John often asks students to refer to specific documents in the folder in order to write a journal entry or to complete a class activity. In another case, a technical writing instructor asks that students submit, along with each final product, a complete record of the writing process that led to that product. Students are expected to keep — within reason — hard copies of all of their notes, drafts, outlines, peer reviews, and photocopied articles to show the instructor evidence of their discovery, drafting, and research processes. The key feature of a writing folder is that it includes *everything* related to a project or course, and the contents demonstrate how much collecting, drafting, and revising the writer has done.

- **A learning or open portfolio** Not necessarily submitted for assessment purposes, this type of portfolio gives students the opportunity to submit a variety of materials that have contributed to their learning of the course material or subject matter. In this approach, students are free to determine the portfolio's contents and how the contents will be presented or organized. Keepers of learning portfolios may choose a variety of documents to demonstrate what and how they learned, including photos or both print and nonprint artifacts. For example, in a course on writing with computers, Sara requests that students' learning portfolios be submitted electronically, but other than that, students are free to make all of the choices. Students can choose to send their Web page addresses, copies of online correspondence with others, or transcripts of online discussions in which they participated, in addition to their more formal writing assignments. Open portfolios work well for a variety of courses, not just writing courses. For example, Sheila keeps a learning portfolio for her beginning ballet class. She includes a videotape of her work at the barre during the second week, seventh week, and fifteenth week, and she writes an accompanying explanation of the improvements her instructor should notice. She also submits a journal, written for herself in twice-weekly entries, about her sore legs, blistered toes, and improved posture as well as her elation at being praised in class for the first time. Sheila's learning portfolio also includes a research paper on the dancer Natalia Makarova and a ticket stub from a performance by the American Ballet Theatre. Sheila's learning portfolio for her ballet class is not limited to written materials, to projects assigned by the instructor, or to activities done in class. She chooses a variety of items that demonstrate *how* she learned (not just *what* she learned) in beginning ballet.

- **A closed portfolio** Often used for assessment purposes, this type of portfolio gives writers considerable guidance in what to submit. Students may have fewer choices or options but still need to make decisions, to show as much variety as possible within the guidelines, and to demonstrate their ability to look critically on their work. For example, for an introductory American literature course, the instructor asks each student to submit these items: (1) a revision of the comparison/contrast essay on two short stories; (2) an explication of an unassigned contemporary poem in the anthology; and (3) one of the two essay exams written in class (the actual blue book), along with an explanation of how the student would rewrite the exam or change his or her responses. As a preface to their three portfolio entries, students are asked to explain their choices and to make a case for what they have learned about American literature. From the portfolios, submitted in the last week of classes, the instructor will create the final exam questions.

- **A midterm portfolio** Students are able to give the portfolio method a trial run, or one or two papers are submitted for evaluation, perhaps accompanied by a brief self-assessment, to determine the midterm grade. For example, in a research writing course designed around collaborative projects, the instructor requests a midterm portfolio instead of a midterm exam. Each group is asked to write a collaborative proposal to the instructor via e-mail about which assignment they will be entering and why. After receiving their instructor's approval to submit their informative paper about changes in libraries in the last five years, Group 1 revises and edits in response to comments received from the instructor and the other groups. Group 1 then writes a brief statement to the class about what their submission demonstrates about their increasing understanding of research. Finally, Group 1 submits the midterm portfolio electronically to the course Web page, where all of the students in the course will be able to read the group's submission and make comments.

- **A final or presentation portfolio** At the end of the course, each student submits a portfolio — revised, edited, and polished to presentation quality — and it is evaluated to determine a significant portion of their final grade. (This type of portfolio may overlap with the closed portfolio or other types, but the difference is the emphasis on *polish*.) For instance, with three weeks remaining in the term, Jeff asks students to review their working folders carefully, charting the contents and choosing those pieces that they are most interested in revising. Then Jeff asks students to write a revision plan for one of those pieces. Next, in a group conference, students discuss some of their choices and revision plans, hear the ideas of others, and begin putting together their final portfolios. In one of the last class meetings before the portfolio is due, students meet in workshop groups to read and respond to one another's reflective introductions.

- **A modified or combination portfolio** Many portfolio designs fall under this category, as this type offers some choices but also outlines requirements to fulfill. The portfolio keeper makes some choices within certain boundaries. In my first-year composition courses, for example, a typical portfolio requirement is that students keep a writing folder throughout the term; then they choose which three writing projects (out of five or six) they wish to revise and edit for portfolio presentation. Along with the three projects, students choose from the writing folder any three to five pages that best represent their learning or their writing strengths, improvement, or interests. These three to five pages may be brief in-class writings, journal entries, postwrites, or reading response pieces, and the selections will vary for each student, giving the portfolio variety and individuality. This portfolio assignment is "open" in that students choose what pieces to include, but it is also "closed" in that I ask for a specific number of entries. For my upper-division courses in writing, I allow students more freedom to design their final portfolio. Instead of asking for three projects, revised and polished, I let students propose what they want to include, and we discuss, as a class, what is enough and what is too much. The choices students make about what to include are informed by what they have learned about audience, purpose, voice, and other elements of the rhetorical situation.

Before exploring further all of the opportunities or options portfolios offer for writing courses, and certainly before making firm decisions about the features, emphases, and pace of your own portfolio courses, you might want to think about portfolios from a very personal perspective and to try to practice the same kind of portfolio keeping that you're going to ask of students. In the next chapter, then, I encourage teachers to become more reflective about their own practices, beginning with the idea of a teacher portfolio.

— 2 —
Portfolio Teaching and Reflective Practice

Do you stuff everything concerning your teaching life in folders, a drawer, or a box? You might even have every syllabus, assignment sheet, or photocopied handout from all the courses you've taught, and they might be organized neatly in file drawers or in labeled files on your hard drive. You have saved, kept, and filed — now this section invites you to spend some time reflecting on what it all *means*.

The principles of portfolio keeping don't change much, whatever the audience or purpose; that is, choice, variety, and reflection are the dominant characteristics of any portfolio created in an educational setting. Therefore, teaching portfolios need to illustrate the portfolio keepers' choices, the variety of materials they found helpful or valuable, and evidence of reflection on their teaching practices.

Reflection is, along with choice and variety, one of the fundamental portfolio principles. For teaching with portfolios, reflection becomes even more important; it is the principle of portfolio keeping that carries over into portfolio teaching. I begin with reflection and with teacher portfolios because keeping your own portfolio is perhaps the best way to guide students with their portfolios, and because there can be personal benefits for you that range from the very practical to the more idealistic.

WHY KEEP A TEACHING PORTFOLIO?

Although they are commonly referred to in the literature as teaching portfolios, a better name might be *learning portfolios for teachers*, because the idea or goal is to learn from the experience — to learn about yourself as a teacher and (sometimes) to convey those realizations to others. A teaching portfolio can be used

1. for a job change or promotion;
2. to provide a model for students, teachers-in-training, or interested colleagues (the "practice what we preach" reason);
3. to record a teaching history; or
4. to become a better teacher.

Teaching portfolios are often discussed in the context of training new teachers, and this connection is important (see, for example, Anson 1994;

Yagelski 1977; Burch 1997; Weiser 1997). Portfolios give learners room, and for those learning about teaching, portfolios offer the space to explore projects, pose questions, express anxieties, and even anticipate disasters. As part of a course for preservice teachers or new graduate teaching assistants, portfolios can provide a packet of materials that new teachers can draw on later in practical ways, but portfolio keeping can also become a routine practice for new teachers, shaping their reflective teaching for years to come (Gaughn 1997, 203–12). Teaching portfolios can also be shared or made available as references, helping new teachers to see the many forms portfolios can take and to give them a set of options for personalizing their portfolios.

Portfolios for practicing teachers and active professionals might take different forms or serve different purposes, but the elements of choice, variety, and reflection don't change. One obvious and practical purpose for the portfolio is as a job-search tool — its contents serve to introduce the candidate to prospective employers. A related purpose is to prepare a portfolio to make a case for promotion or advancement. This use of portfolios is becoming more common: The 1998 MLA Job Information List contains several job ads asking for teaching portfolios, and the National Board for Professional Teaching Standards, a year-long assessment and certification process, includes a portfolio of five months of teaching. In these cases, the portfolio's purpose is a persuasive one, and it is intended for those who have some power over the portfolio keeper/presenter.

These types of collections — the tenure packets or career dossiers — allow us to illustrate our accomplishments or our approaches to teaching, to explain what's included by providing context and history, and of course to brag in a fairly sophisticated way. Reflection may be a part of our process in choosing the materials, but perhaps not part of the final product.

Reflection is necessary, however, in both the process and product of a teacher's learning portfolio, and the audience for the choices, variety, and reflection may be the "self" rather than supervisors, evaluators, or others. While the best reasons for practicing teachers to keep and maintain a portfolio may seem less immediately practical than a dossier, the long-term benefits include having always at hand important "artifacts" related to one's career and cultivating a habit of reflection that carries over into all of one's teaching practices. The habit of reflection is a hard habit to break. Every assignment, explanation, presentation, or approach comes under thoughtful scrutiny: "Is this the best way to . . . ?" "Should I spend more time on . . . ?" "Was there enough discussion today about . . . ?" Keeping a portfolio gives us teachers the same kind of experiences we're asking of students; it also helps us to become more attuned to the nuances of learning and more flexible about ways to assess performance.

STARTING YOUR TEACHING (LEARNING) PORTFOLIO

Start keeping! If you have file drawers or storage space, for either electronic or paper files, you probably have more than enough raw material with which to begin. Before you start sorting and choosing what goes in and what doesn't and why, some planning might help, as may narrowing the purpose to one area of your teaching life, especially if you are an experienced teacher. What materials best represent whatever area of your teaching life you want to record, explore, or share? How much is too much?

Like any writing project, a key to your decisions will be finding a purpose and audience (real or imagined) that inspires other decisions. If your purpose is not to change jobs or land a promotion, what reasons for a teaching portfolio might shape your choices, and what audience might influence your collection?

Possible Purposes

- To remind you of the hours, days, weeks, and years you've devoted to teaching
- To reminisce about past classes, students, and moments
- To keep track of changes you've made or risks you've taken
- To leave a record of your career

Possible Audiences — Real or Imagined, Addressed or Invoked

- Other experienced teachers you respect — those whose works you've read; those you've heard present lectures; those whose classes you wish you could take, or take again
- Your own students, graduate or undergraduate, present or future or past
- Your favorite colleagues in your department, at regional meetings, or at national conferences
- People who are important to you but who don't really know you as a teacher or who don't see you in action — family members and close friends

Once you have a purpose and audience in mind, the next step is to be selective and reflective — to be conscious about what you choose to present and why. What follows is certainly no recipe but merely a list of suggestions for a portfolio intended to demonstrate to others (administrators or supervisors) one's teaching experience and ability:

- A "packet" for a course you teach often, including a course description and sample syllabus; assignments; in-class activities; and a few examples of the student writing produced in that course

- Another packet or set of materials for a course you've prepared and taught once but haven't been able to teach again (included might be ideas for how you would teach the course a second time, as many of us want at least two shots at a course — the first time to experiment and the second to tighten or sharpen)
- A list of all courses taught, with a bit of information about each
- A curriculum vitae, or a résumé
- A statement of teaching philosophy or teaching methods
- Materials for a professional presentation you gave on some teaching topic

Prefacing or concluding all of this, of course, or introducing each section, should be a piece that situates the contents and reflects on what it all means to you, the learner. This reflective piece has no required or expected form; cover letters are common, but they are by no means the only option. The contents of the portfolio will be more meaningful, especially to others, if there is an introduction of some kind, but depending on the purpose and audience, that piece could be anything and should invite creativity and risk taking.

WHAT'S IN MY TEACHING PORTFOLIO

I started my teaching portfolio when I was having an "uninspired" semester. All three of my undergraduate writing classes were a bit on the dull or flat side, and I needed to know how much of it was me. In my umpteenth year of teaching writing, I worried that I was becoming the proverbial bored and disenchanted tenured professor. I joined a teaching seminar (the Instructional Development Program) available at my institution, where twenty faculty members across the disciplines meet twice a month to discuss assigned readings, to try out collaborative learning activities, to listen to presentations by accomplished teachers, and to share a meal. These "teaching fellows" became part of my audience for my teaching portfolio, but another part of my audience was *me*: I wanted to shake off my teaching blues and reestablish my sense of self as a teacher. My portfolio included:

- A list of all the different types of courses I've taught, along with brief descriptions of each, beginning with a first-year composition course at Emporia State University in 1983, a course I taught with Maxine Hairston's *A Contemporary Rhetoric* (third edition), the standard textbook.
- The syllabus, bibliography, reserve lists, handouts, and assignment sheets from the first graduate course in rhetorical theory I taught, in 1991, next to the same materials for the most recent graduate course I designed, for the fall of 1998.
- A packet of my favorite essay assignments from many years of teaching first-year composition, including some that I now find dated or too prescriptive.

- A few selections from teaching journals I've kept, mostly entries that keep me humble. One was written after a particularly frustrating class meeting when I was trying to use "typical" collaborative group work in a writing class that had *both* native and nonnative speakers. (What was I thinking?) Others are included from the writing I do in class with my students.

- A list of my favorite books and articles about teaching writing. This list includes Donald Murray's *A Writer Teaches Writing*, Nancie Atwell's *In the Middle*, Adrienne Rich's "Teaching Language in Open Admissions"; and bell hooks's *Teaching to Transgress*.

- Copies of some letters of recommendation I've written for students over the years — undergraduates headed for medical school, M.A. students seeking admission to a doctoral program — and some thank-you notes and cards.

I would prepare a very different teaching portfolio if I were applying for promotion or a new position, but *my* teaching portfolio is mostly *for me*, to remind me of where I've been as a teacher and what's important to me about teaching writing. I look at it when I need reminders or encouragement or a sense of a teaching past.

Even those portfolio teachers who choose not to be portfolio *keepers* will find their teaching experience enhanced or enriched by acts of reflection. I have three ideas about how to practice reflection in ways other than portfolio keeping (or in addition to portfolio keeping), but there are undoubtedly others.

Other Ways for Teachers to Practice Reflection

1. Keep a teaching journal. We ask our students to keep reading response journals or to free-write about class discussions, assignments, or activities. We can do the same, and many of us *do* write with our students. To be more reflective and more systematic about these kinds of writing, record them in the same notebook or folder each time, compiling many of these entries over time, and periodically read and review the entries, looking for patterns, parallels, or insights. In reading or writing our own teaching logs, we can make connections, interpret situations, and discern meaning.

2. Join a teaching group or special-interest group. Many campuses have teaching specialists, "master teachers," instructional development programs, or faculty reading or writing groups. While not all of these may focus on teaching, being professionally active can make us more reflective about our learning habits, preferences, or interests.

3. Conduct small-scale teacher research. Nothing enhances one's skills of keen observation, note taking, and organizing materials like conducting a study, even a small one. Although teacher research or action research is far too involved to treat adequately here (and I don't want to treat it too casually), I do want to mention it as an excellent strategy for reflective teaching, with or without the goal of dissemination or publication. Using qualitative methods, in particular, forces the responsible researcher into a position of reflection — a stance from which one views the classroom in a fresh light, from a different angle. Reflection in this case means being accountable for one's own position in the classroom. It means asking such questions as, "Why am I so invested in . . . ?" My own most recent teacher-research project was to study my students' portfolio introductions and my own reading habits for those documents. (For more information on teacher research, see Ray 1993; Daiker and Morenberg 1990.)

Reflective practice in our writing courses can make us keenly aware of the situations we are putting students in, or of what we are asking of them intellectually when we ask them to keep a portfolio and to reflect on its contents. Portfolios change or evolve according to different situations or purposes, so one place to start with portfolio preparation is to try to analyze or understand the rhetorical context.

—3—
Portfolio Preparation as a Rhetorical Act

I value portfolios for the ways in which they ask students to make rhetorically informed choices and to be responsible for those choices in a "real" situation. One of the biggest challenges of teaching "school" writing, especially in required composition courses, is getting students to see that the writing is "real" and not just invented for the purposes of, well, required writing courses. Students recognize that school-sponsored writing is often written only for the teacher or doesn't resemble the kinds of writing they see in the "real world" (although service learning and civic discourse are beginning to close this gap). While, ideally, writers find or determine their own reasons for writing, the nature of writing for college credit requires us to supply some of the "urgency" for our students. Portfolio writing courses achieve this urgency or meaningfulness by balancing process and product with two equally important rhetorical situations: the process of learning and the product for assessment. Portfolios, while still very clearly "school-sponsored," provide an exigence that traditional writing assignments may not because of the way the process of portfolio keeping builds to a moment of portfolio evaluation.

   Through their dual function of recording a learning process and assessing a final product, portfolios give students tangible rhetorical situations that allow them, first, to practice, develop, grow, or take risks, and then, when the time is right, to perform, to pull it all together, to show their stuff. When the portfolio comes due at the end of the course and is worth a large percentage of a course grade, suddenly lessons about rhetoric matter. But the portfolio process *before* assessment can also be richly rhetorical.

Portfolios give us great opportunities to reinforce rhetorical concepts or principles that inform — consciously or not — all writers' processes. Our goal should be to find ways, first, to make the whole process of portfolio preparation richly rhetorical and, second, to make portfolio assessment an inviting rhetorical situation that students can enter into. In this chapter, I make a case for the rhetorical nature of portfolios and suggest ways that the pedagogical practice of portfolios might connect to the more theoretical content of our courses: rhetoric. In both the process of keeping and the product of presentation, portfolios give a new spin to the following rhetorical principles or concepts: situation, habit and responsibility, self-presentation, arrangement, and audience.

SITUATION

The portfolio class is not "more" rhetorical than others, but it does afford opportunities of situation that traditional process-driven classes might not. For example, there's a dramatic buildup to the course or term, much like several weeks of play practice before the dress rehearsal and then opening night. As the working folder expands and the time to select entries draws nearer, portfolio classrooms take on an exciting atmosphere. Students know that the time for summative evaluation is near, and some of the buzz is certainly due to how much the portfolio "counts." Students seem to like the fact that they have the full term to "get better," and they also look forward to the evaluation and to the sharing, but when the portfolio is worth a large percentage of their final course grade, anxiety is often part of the mix. The situation is more like writing in the workplace or like professional writing in that projects often require weeks for development, but the stakes are often quite high in terms of the writer's success.

As a part of a process writing classroom that emphasizes the importance of a final product, portfolios cause a palpable difference in atmosphere in the writing classroom, and teachers can take advantage of the situation to reinforce lessons about rhetoric. How does it change writers' strategies to have so much time to revise and polish, for example? How does time change the stakes or alter the approach? Students can be asked to analyze the rhetorical situation of portfolio keeping by contrasting it with other writing situations or predicting how different time constraints would affect the outcome. The situation for presentation or assessment is affected by timing as well as writing program policies, the content or emphases of the course, and the particular style, preferences, or personality of the instructor. Students try to identify some of these factors and ask, "How does this affect my portfolio choices?"

If students can cultivate the habit of always weighing their choices, then they will be more rhetorically prepared for other situations and other choices.

HABIT AND RESPONSIBILITY

In classical rhetoric, a speaker's ethical appeal depended on his character. The ancients understood that character was formed through habit or habitual practices — from "the company one keeps" to how one spends time. Good habits — intellectual and physical — resulted in good character, and, in turn, an effective ethos. Rhetors who lacked good habits or who did not live habitually well could not be trusted or had a poor ethos. The word *ethos* and the word *habit* in Greek share a root, in fact, and the same root connects to the word for place, space, or haunt. Habits are formed — as character is also formed — in the places where one lives, works, and hangs out. If we think of portfolios, metaphorically, as a place where writers work, we can also imagine that the habitual nature of their upkeep and maintenance contributes to the character formation of engaged and careful writers.

The writing process movement reclaimed habit as an important principle of good writing. *Nulla dies sine linea* ("Not a day without a line"), from Pliny the Elder in the first century, became Donald Murray's mantra in his published articles of the late 1960s and early 1970s. Murray's ethos as a writing instructor and writing professional was formed, in part, through his public sharing of his writing logs, the place where his written pieces began to take shape — the same place where his character was formed. In public performances with an overhead projector and a marker pen or grease pencil, Murray took the risk of composing aloud, with an audience, to show teacher-writers how they might demonstrate the processes of writing to their students.

The habit of portfolio keeping is rhetorical because portfolios demand a certain amount of vigilance and responsibility; portfolio learners must pay attention and must treat the portfolio as a process that leads to a product. When it's time to prepare that product, the habits that each writer has developed will affect his or her self-presentation.

SELF-PRESENTATION

Connected to habit is the concept of the appeal from character, or what we might call self-presentation. How do portfolio learners present themselves to readers? Some of this self-presentation is clearly connected (again) to choices: How does Virginia choose to describe herself as a writer, learner, or student? How does Paul refer to his writing habits or preferences? Is the self-presentation explicit or implicit, or how much of himself or herself does the writer reveal?

Because the entire portfolio can be seen as a presentation of self — with evidence of the writer's understanding of everything from argument to manuscript format — it's difficult to separate the "ethos" from other appeals or other persuasive elements. That's one of the reasons portfolios are evaluated holistically, as a package deal.

ARRANGEMENT

The second canon of classical rhetoric, following invention, arrangement addresses the problem of "selecting and marshalling the available material" to effect one's purpose (Corbett 1999, 256). As rhetoricians advise, writers have to select "what is most pertinent and cogent." Even the best material, carefully chosen with the best of reasons, will fail to achieve its purpose without order (256). Writers choose how to organize their working folders — where to put each document or page and what to call things or how to label them. In the portfolio presentation, writers arrange the portfolio according to their judgment about what pieces would be most effective first, second, third, and so on. While some of the arrangement may be assigned by the instructor — perhaps a requirement that the reflective essay comes first — students still have some choices to make about arranging the contents of both the working folder and the final portfolio. Students may need to be coached about how to anticipate the consequences or implications of their arrangement, or about the best relationship between the parts and the sequence. The importance of arrangement reminds us, too, that we emphasize "introductions" and conclusions and the other parts of essays for very good reasons — because those parts are intricately tied to audience, purpose, and subject matter. Portfolios, if treated as a whole discourse, need an introduction, for example, that prepares readers for the subject at hand. Even if the introduction is not the reflective element, there needs to be an introduction to a portfolio and perhaps a conclusion as well.

AUDIENCE

Teacher-graded classroom portfolios offer the same audience for students as do traditional writing assignments — that is, the teacher will be grading this — but portfolio teachers have found ways to expand, enlarge, or shift student writers' sense of audience from the classroom teacher to a "bigger place." First, as in most process writing classes, collaboration shifts the sense of audience from the teacher to other (peer) readers. When writers work together from the invention stage through revision and editing, students begin to make choices from a broader perspective or to realize the different ways those choices might be read or interpreted. Also, some teachers will arrange to grade one another's portfolios — perhaps in a trial run at midterm — to give writers the sense of another reader and how their work is read by someone outside the class. (This collaborative way of evaluating portfolios formed the basis of the portfolio writing program that Pat Belanoff and Peter Elbow developed.) More recently, portfolio instructors are discovering the possibilities that the Internet offers for expanding writers' conceptions of audience: By posting essays or projects to the Web, where the Web site might be read by anyone, students begin to realize the importance of choices and the responsibilities of being "an author."

Even without these expanded senses of audience, the process of portfolios, especially their built-in revision, helps to cultivate and reinforce the habits of thinking about readers' needs. Students don't need another audience besides the teacher to learn something about audience, choices, and responsibility.

Generally, then, portfolios provide a solid foundation for a writing course that emphasizes rhetoric, and teachers need to make choices, early in the course planning, about ways to emphasize the rhetorical nature of portfolios. The portfolio habit encourages, most of all, responsible, self-conscious ways of making choices. To present a successful portfolio, whatever the goals or guidelines of the portfolio situation, writers must show that they can keep the situation and audience in mind, incorporating, where necessary or appropriate, appeals to reason, to character, or to emotion.

The portfolio product or final portfolio provides an even richer rhetorical situation for readers and writers, an "occasion" that brings readers and writers together with a common goal. The whole portfolio is, in fact, a persuasive document. It is evaluated according to its ability to persuade its readers/evaluators that the portfolio keeper has exercised good judgment, displayed sound thinking, anticipated readers, learned the subject matter of the course, revised judiciously, and edited carefully.

—4—
Course Planning and
Routine Activities

The portfolio process, like the writing process, is recursive (not linear), messy (not tidy), often disjointed (not unified). Portfolios put a particular spin on the writing process classroom, but they are not at all at odds with the typical activities of many writing classrooms, which emphasize time, ownership, and response (Atwell 1998), or collaboration and revision. Teaching with portfolios *may* require some adjustments in organizing the course, or more flexibility. Generally, incorporating portfolios often means that a few other things might change: the course's pace, order of events, or emphases.

Like any writing course, the portfolio course improves with experience and benefits from planning, but **a portfolio method works best if planned in**

advance and introduced on the first day of class. Sometimes when I talk about portfolios with teachers, especially inexperienced ones, they get very excited and want to incorporate them right away, regardless of whether it's Week 5 or Week 12 of the semester. I suggest that they hang on to their enthusiasm but wait until they have the fresh start of a new course. Although portfolios are very flexible and adaptable, they are not a last-minute pedagogy, and portfolio teaching is a whole package. Thus, the portfolio process needs to be woven into the fabric of the course because portfolios create a unique rhetorical situation.

Students should hear about their portfolios during the first day of class, find information on them in the syllabus or course outline, and get their first reading assignments from *Portfolio Keeping*. This chapter reviews what planning or decisions need to happen in advance and addresses elements of a writing course particularly affected by the introduction of portfolios.

Questions to Anticipate

- What goes in my portfolio?
- Can short, informal pieces be included? If so, how much revision and editing do they need? Can I include a journal entry without changing it at all?
- How much does my portfolio count?
- How will it be graded?
- Will *you* be grading it?
- Will you count improvement or effort?

It's a good idea, of course, to have rehearsed answers to such questions for the first day of class, but students may not have questions until the course is well under way and they have a better sense of what to ask. Therefore, I recommend spending some class time at midterm and at the three-quarter semester mark giving students a chance to ask questions about the portfolio in class discussion and in writing.

GENERAL GUIDELINES FOR ASSIGNING THE PORTFOLIO

In making sound rhetorical choices, students need to work within the guidelines you have set, so make sure they know these guidelines in plenty of time to start choosing entries and revising. It's not easy to find ways to give students structure without limiting their (rhetorical) choices — or to know how to plan carefully enough to leave room for flexibility, spontaneity, and surprises — but I believe that students do need some structure.

First, your syllabus should, of course, include at least a paragraph on the portfolio, briefly explaining its importance and its role in the course and how much it counts in the final grade. Details or depth aren't necessary, but it's important to let students know that the portfolio is the end product, the culmination of their efforts, and that it will contain their "best" work. If you will be *assigning* a working folder, explain it briefly, too, and remind students to bring it to every class meeting. Students need to know that you will do quick checks, periodically, to see that they are keeping the contents of their folders up to date, organized, and labeled.

Here are the most basic guidelines you'll need to decide on: What can or should be included, and what are the expectations for the "condition" of the contents? Can students choose to include brief response papers, position papers, reaction papers, or one-minute papers? Can they include journal entries? impromptu or timed writings done in class? If so, is revision expected? optional? not required? Is editing expected? optional? Many of your students' decisions will hinge on these guidelines.

In my first-year composition courses, students keep a working folder and write five "projects" or essays. From the total production of their semester's work, I require that three of the five projects — their choice — be revised and polished for the final portfolio, along with up to five additional pages of any writing they wish to include. Those five pages can come from five postwrites, from the peer response forms, from journal entries or impromptu pieces composed in class, from e-mail correspondence, or from the two remaining projects. Whatever students choose for those additional entries, they must make a case for their choices in the reflective introduction — to be able to say why the entries are there and what they illustrate. In addition, the portfolio is made up of only clean, final, polished copies; it is a presentation portfolio and not a folder of writings.

For other writing courses, the guidelines vary according to the course material and the emphases of the various assignments. In a creative nonfiction class, for example, students are free to choose what to include — again, as long as they make a good case for their decisions in the introduction. I do remind students about the importance of variety, and students are expected to provide a rationale for their choices during or after the "time-to-decide" conference (discussed in Chapter 7 of this book).

If I were teaching a content-specific writing course such as business or technical writing, I might specify more carefully what students should include or give them more restrictions — not to inhibit their freedom but to make clear the course's values and expectations. In any case, you'll need to decide on and specify what your students' options and responsibilities are, from within a range of guidelines.

SCHEDULING AND PACE

In the first two to three weeks of the term, a few things need to be covered or established: (1) outlining the portfolio method in the syllabus; (2) getting students into a routine of keeping their working folder, starting their journal, or practicing self-assessment; and (3) assigning the first section of *Portfolio Keeping*.

For most of the term, students are busy starting new essays, preparing for each writing workshop, reading assigned materials and one another's drafts, and maintaining their working folders. During these weeks, the routine of the course may not vary much, and students may need an occasional reminder about the portfolio because it fades, for a while, as the production cycle is high.

The portfolio moves into the center of the course after the last essay or project has been "completed." With approximately two or three weeks left in the term, no new major projects should be assigned so that students can devote the remainder of the term to the portfolio: choosing, revising, editing, polishing, reflecting, and writing the introduction or reflective essay. At this point, then, as students really face the portfolio task head-on, class time should be devoted to a thorough review of expectations and procedures. Students will not have many questions in the first week, but in Week 12, they will have plenty. This is the time to discuss relevant parts from *Portfolio Keeping* (Chapters 6–9) and to schedule time-to-decide conferences. At least one class period, too, should be devoted to a workshop for the reflective introduction or essay.

During most of a term, routine activities of a portfolio writing class do not differ from the routine activities of a class without portfolios. Here's a routine that my undergraduate writing classes typically follow:

Week 1	Assign new project (Project 3)	Group invention/ a writing prompt	Discussion of reading
Week 2	Progress reports/ more reading to discuss	Writing workshop	Revised version due to me/postwrites and editing done in class
Week 3	Project 4 assigned/ discussion of reading	Group invention or library work	(a week later) Project 3 returned with comments toward revision and a graded postwrite

Unlike "typical" process writing classes, time must be allotted for revision of the portfolio entries. Incorporating portfolios means leaving time at the end of the term for the revision and preparation of the final portfolio. If each project takes approximately two weeks to complete, then the last project should be assigned with about four weeks left in the semester. This way students have time to complete that last project while you have time to respond and return it; then the last papers can also be considered for inclusion in the portfolio. Although there are several variables for how much time to allow, I give students about two weeks for the following activities:

- Deciding which projects to revise, edit, and polish for the portfolio — and deciding how much attention each needs (NOTE: if not every piece needs to be revised or edited and polished, then less time is required)

- Completing the revision and editing needed for each entry
- Planning, drafting, and completing the writing process for the reflective introduction
- Preparing the final manuscript of the entire portfolio, including formatting or document design, editing, proofreading, and so forth

OTHER CONSIDERATIONS FOR
COURSE PLANNING

While portfolio writing classes do not differ in the day-to-day activities from a process writing class, I want to make three suggestions, in particular, that I hope will make your portfolio course more successful.

Assign Plenty of Writing

This may seem self-evident. Of course students need to produce a lot of writing in a writing course. But as process teaching increased the numbers of drafts instructors were expected to read, and as overworked and undervalued instructors have struggled to meet the demands of delivering the curriculum, large composition programs have asked for fewer (formal) papers or projects. When I started teaching at my present institution in 1991, the College Writing Program required seven papers or projects in the standard syllabus for Writing 101. A few years later, in response to complaints from weary graduate teaching assistants and instructors, the number of required projects was lowered to six. Now it is five. True, the standard syllabus also encourages generous use of brief, informal writings or some writing-to-learn pieces in addition to the major projects — for example, journals, reading-response papers, in-class prompts, and so on. But students who write five projects have fewer choices when deciding on portfolio entries than do those who have written seven. The options? More, shorter papers may fit better with a portfolio method. Instead of five three-to-seven page projects, for example, portfolio instructors may choose to assign ten two-page papers, with the best five of these expanded for the portfolio. Or, in lieu of more assignments, instructors can also invite students to include in the portfolio their best or representative examples of journal entries, reading-response papers, and other quick, informal (ungraded) writings. If teachers and students have some flexibility within their curriculums, they can fulfill the portfolio principles of choice and variety.

Practice All Kinds of Assessment,
but Don't Grade Everything

Portfolios encourage "more" writing — so that students will have choices to make — but teachers don't have to "grade" all of it. As the preceding section suggests, one of the best ways to provide choice and variety is to give students dozens of opportunities to write. For teachers to grade all of these writings would be both impossible and detrimental, so one of the most important aspects of course planning is to schedule time for response and to expand our traditional notions of responding to student writing. Given the demands of responding and grading, in a portfolio course or any other writing-intensive course, I devote much of Chapters 6 and 9 to these concerns. For now, however, let me share this anecdote. When I have used taped responses, instead of written comments, I haven't mentioned a grade in my oral comments; I've given ideas for how students might revise the paper should they choose to pursue it. Even without my mentioning a letter grade, however, students have routinely reported that they "could tell" how I felt about a paper just by my tone of voice. As I suggested changes or commented on the effect of certain passages, then, students picked up cues about how they were doing, through signals of word choice, pitch, and intonation — signs I wasn't aware I was sending. Students, therefore, *hear* "assessment messages" even when you're not consciously sending them. Students associate teachers so firmly with assessment, evaluation, or grades, that they hear assessment in everything that you suggest to them. Communication with them as reader to writers, not just as teacher to students, is difficult to establish. Therefore, I try to "surprise" them whenever possible, by *not* putting a grade on most of what they write.

Make Reflection Routine

Perhaps the most important consideration when planning a portfolio writing course is to incorporate plenty of opportunities for reflective learning — to make reflection a habitual, routine part of the course. A reflective element to the course need not be elaborate: It might be regular in-class writing that asks both students and teacher to pause and take stock of, for example, that day's class or the most recent assignment.

Although complicated reflective assignments are not necessary, becoming a reflective learner does take time and practice. Students need to practice reflection before it "counts," before the portfolio is due with a reflective component. Therefore, it's better to begin cultivating a reflective writing process very early in the course, and teachers need to provide opportunities for reflective learning throughout the course so that students are not asked to produce it, for the first time, when the stakes are high.

To this end, it's a good idea to inaugurate the course with a reflective activity so that students begin right away to develop their own understanding of what we mean by reflective learning. Instead of handing them definitions or models, I give them the following writing prompt, a version of which is found in *Portfolio Keeping*:

> Please review carefully the course syllabus I just gave you, paying careful attention to the course policies, procedures, assignments, and expectations. Next, go buy the required books and review them, too. Finally, think about your impressions of this class after our first meeting today. Drawing on those three sources of data — the syllabus, the books, and our first meeting — write two paragraphs

about **how you think you will do in this course.** What assignments or activities look familiar, self-explanatory, or manageable, and why? What assignments or activities do you think will be hard for you, and why? What parts of your reading and writing history make you confident about some parts of the course and hesitant about others?

This task is not easy: Ultimately, I'm asking students to draw on materials, documents, or evidence — as well as their own experiences, habits, and attitudes — to make and support a claim. I don't put a letter grade on this assignment, but because expectations (on both sides) are often put into place with a first assignment, I feel it's critical to give students feedback about this short piece they write for the second class meeting. Have students shown some ability to make connections between the course materials they see and their own tendencies as learners or students? I look for specificity, most of all. If students write generic claims ("I think I will do OK in this course because I write pretty well") or statements that lack support from the materials they have been asked to examine (the books, syllabus, and so on), then I point out that they have missed the point of the reflection or haven't said nearly enough. If students answer only the part in boldface type and don't bother referring to the materials, or don't extend their responses into answering "why," then I comment on what's missing. Students often write what I call a "cheerleading" passage, in which they try to show me that they will try, try, try to do their best, that they are prepared to work hard, and that if they take their time, they can succeed. I'm inclined to comment positively about their enthusiasm or confidence, but I also ask where their confidence comes from. That's the hard part of this task for first-year college students: to be "meta-cognitive" or to be able to think about their own thinking. Because of the difficulty of reflection, the next chapter covers it in more detail, with additional ideas for incorporating reflective assignments or activities into the course.

— 5 —

The Reflective Learning Habit

In addition to the first-day prompt of the previous chapter, assignments throughout the course can emphasize for students the importance of reflection and give them chances to practice. Several different approaches can get to the same goals, but the idea is to institute routine or ongoing assignments that get students to practice and cultivate reflective learning — that help them to establish the reflective habit that might influence their learning for

Syllabus
- about me essay.
- write a short story
Short Story
- Odyssey like story.
- Romeo and Juliet Story.
- fan fiction
- Persuasive essay
- reflective
Ceo Summary
Letters.
- Companion Peices for each
- Past writes for each.

years to come. Here's how one experienced portfolio teacher incorporated reflection into her English "methods" course for preservice classroom teachers. Kathleen Yancey writes,

> I emphasized reflection, seeing it not so much as something that came at the end of the portfolio process, as is so often the case (Conway 1994), but as something that threaded throughout the course, in multiple forms and for multiple intents. I asked students to write me biweekly *reflective letters* in which they commented on anything that seemed germane; I asked them to write *goal statements* at the beginning of the class and to revisit those goals periodically; I asked them to write what I called *Learning Summaries*, in which they commented on their learning and how it was progressing; I asked them throughout the term to choose portfolio exhibits and write one-page *rationales* for those exhibits; and I asked students to write a culminating *reflective essay* for their teacher portfolio. ("Teacher Portfolios" 1997, 247; italics in original)

This passage illustrates the variety of forms that reflection can take in writing classes as well as the importance of routine, regular, well-integrated assignments. Students can practice reflection in a variety of ways or forms, but it is not enough just to give them a prompt occasionally that asks them to "reflect on their learning." Developing good prompts or assignments will improve the quality of the reflective entries or will give students some guidance about what to say when they are being reflective. Prompts should, ideally, fit with the theme, content, or direction of the course — or with other assignments. For example, if the class is reading memoirs or literacy narratives (for example, excerpts by Richard Rodriguez, Mike Rose, or Linda Brodkey), then ask students to find evidence of reflection in those passages. Where do the authors try to connect their "present selves" to their past, or where do they make connections between the event they are recounting and what they have *learned* from that event?

In addition, if students have spent some time participating in an online discussion or posting entries to a listserv, ask them to read through several of them, and find some patterns in them, or to identify the three or four most provocative entries — and what those entries made them realize or think about.

If students are keeping a journal, or if you have reserved ten minutes of each week's class time for reflective writing, then you might try something like weekly self-reports. Ask students, basically, to sit down once a week or so and think about how the course is going. In terms of learning the course material, what's making sense and what's still confusing? Where have all the successes — or failures — been concentrated? Most important, ask students to offer one example, illustration, or exercise that contributed the most to their understanding of a specific topic, issue, or assignment. For these weekly self-reports, you may ask students to write one or two paragraphs each week recording their observations about the pace and quality of the course, about their own role within it, and about their goals for the upcoming week. These "reports," as well as journal entries or other writings, should be labeled and dated and saved in the working folder (electronic or paper), so that students can look back and trace patterns they see over the course of several weeks. Is there a point at which the entries change in length or development? in content? in emphasis? in tone?

While journal entries or prompts can vary widely and can ask students to be thoughtful about many aspects of the class, reflection is routinely practiced in my courses through writer's postwrites or memos, or through companion pieces. I like the way that postwrites focus students' attention — and mine — on the topic that matters most: their own writing processes and works-in-progress.

WRITER'S POSTWRITES AND
COMPANION PIECES

Postwrites — written "after" the writing — and companion pieces — written to accompany the main piece — ask students to write about "how the writing is going" and give the writer a chance to share information about the piece that readers would not otherwise have access to. These techniques support reflective learning because they ask writers to think consciously about the choices they've made or the process they've followed; they give writers some control over the response process; and they prompt writers to articulate specific questions they have for their "real" readers. (For more, see Sommers 1989.)

Here's how the postwrite works: When writers are ready for response, they answer some questions (in writing) that will guide and situate readers and that will help the writer to discover or identify, for example, key turning points in the process, or ideas that are still undefined, or questions that the writer has for readers. How the writer feels about the draft, what kind of shape it's in, and who influenced the writing are all good postwrite questions. Companion pieces may not be quite so prescriptive or may lack assigned questions, but the idea of encouraging reflection on the primary text — through a secondary text — is the same. Kathleen Blake Yancey asks students to write companion pieces, for example, based on a heuristic developed from Peter Elbow's doubting game and believing game (Yancey 1998, 31–40).

With either a postwrite or a companion piece, or with some other heuristic, writers need to do some work engaging with and judging their own writing before they ask others to engage or to judge.

On a very practical note, postwrites can help peer response sessions move along more quickly, especially if time is limited, or teacher-readers can gauge more accurately how much a writer struggled with writing her paper, for example, before composing a response. Reading a postwrite *before* reading the paper helps tremendously to match the comments with the writer's needs and to avoid repeating what the writer already knows about the paper.

For the writing classes I teach, I distribute postwrite questions at the beginning of each class meeting when drafts are due for my response. I ask writers to take fifteen minutes to complete the postwrite, urging them to give each question their full attention, and I reward up to five points for a good postwrite — one that is thorough, thoughtful, and specific. I tell students not to worry about sentence structure or spelling, but that I will look for an understanding of the assignment, engagement with the writing process, and direct references to their own (the primary) text.

If students write five or six projects during the course, they will complete five or six postwrites. Although the questions vary according to the assigned project and the point in the course, the last question on the postwrite always remains the same: How can I help you most in my response to this paper? What particular parts, passages, or decisions are you unsure about? What are your questions for me as a reader?

A strong response to this postwrite question will be very specific, as in the following:

example:

> I wasn't obvious with the humor, so I'm worried it may not be understood — esp. the passage about the liberal alcohol policies. Do you think kids will get that? Is it apparent it is supposed to be funny? Does the second page kind of lag? The hardest part was keeping in mind that I was writing to a younger audience. I didn't want to talk down to them either. I think (hope) all the transitions are good.

A weak response to this postwrite question will be very brief, vague, or general:

example:

> Tell me if I did a good job explaining the "entire" experience.

Portfolio Keeping contains two sample postwrites, similar to the one on page 28, that take just a few minutes to create for each assignment and can ask students both specific and progressively more sophisticated questions about their writing processes, decisions, and drafts.

I always read the postwrite first, before I read the paper, because the postwrite guides much of my response and makes students partly responsible for the kind of response they receive. For example, if Cheryl's postwrite says, "I love this paper!" I'm going to be particularly careful about how I respond — especially if I see that the essay needs considerable revision. If Mike's postwrite describes a writing process that took all of thirty minutes, I'm going to reconsider whether I should spend twenty minutes on my written commentary. If Janelle's postwrite shows how frustrated she is but also how engaged, I'll try to respond accordingly; if Emil's postwrite asks me what I think about his introduction, that's where I'll start.

With questions that ask for accounts and reflections, postwrites help both writers and readers to get more out of the response process. Postwrite questions, however informal, help writers to identify areas in which they feel dissatisfied with the draft, even if they cannot quite name, let alone "fix," the problem. Once alerted to a fuzzy or weak or dissatisfying area, readers may see exactly what it needs and may suggest something the writer would never have considered. Postwrites also help to train students in responding to the drafts of their peers. Reading a postwrite first will help readers know where to look or will give them a "push" in giving responsible, thorough feedback.

POSTWRITE FOR PROJECT 5: THE REVIEW

Name: _____

Title: _____

1. What did you review and for what target publication? What criteria did you use? Implicit or explicit or both?

2. What did you need to "know" or "do" in order to write this review?

3. What will I find in your folder besides this postwrite and the draft for today? What will your folder's contents tell me about your writing process, your choices or decisions, or your problems/successes with this project?

4. Refer me to a specific passage in which you have used **facts.** Then, refer me to a specific passage in which you have used **description** (with the use of details). Finally, refer me to a specific passage in which you have used **evaluation** (your judgment).

5. As usual, how can I help you most in my response to this paper? What parts are you concerned about, or where are you uncertain about your decisions? Please be specific! What questions do you have for me as a reader?

SAMPLE POSTWRITE

If it is not feasible for you to create and make photocopies of postwrite forms, like the one illustrated, for each class, then the questions can be put on an overhead projector or on the chalkboard, and students can write their responses on notebook paper. Even without several postwrite questions or a fairly structured approach to them, at the very least, writers should be asked to record quickly for each draft what they think the paper does well and what it still needs (Donald Murray helps here: "What works and what *needs* work?"). Students should also be encouraged, if not assigned, to keep track (in notes dated, labeled, and saved) of the process they went through to plan, research, or draft each paper — where they got stuck and where things clicked. These notes will help significantly when students are asked to explain their writing process for a particular paper, or when they are asked — via the portfolio method — to write reflectively about their own learning.

WORKING WITH THE WORKING FOLDER

The reflective learning habit can be established with postwrites or companion pieces, but making good pedagogical use of the working folder will also help students' abilities to reflect. To be an effective learning tool, the working folder must be a part of the class routine, and it must be more than just a place to store drafts. Keeping the working folder up to date and organized is the means to an end: to make the final portfolio steps easier and to help enrich the reflective piece written at the end of the course. Checking that students have the folder with them can be a place to start, as can asking to see it to confirm that they are keeping it organized.

What goes in the working folder? All assignment sheets, notes, lists, drafts, outlines, or freewriting; all peer response forms, returned pieces with marginal and end comments, and postwrites. Students may choose to organize the contents by project — placing everything for the literacy narrative together — or by dates, or by type. For example, they may put all of their postwrites together; all of their early planning pages together; all of their research materials together; and so forth. The point is to encourage a record-keeping system that students can follow independently, and to remind them periodically of the need to review the contents and reflect on the patterns, changes, trends, or habits they see in their work.

It's the students' job to keep their working folder responsibly, but it's our job to guide them in how to use it to improve their writing, learning, or self-reflection. Simply looking at the working folder to "check it" isn't very helpful for students. When it's time to pay some explicit attention to the working folder, students need guidance or structure about how to "see" the contents. They must be prompted to analyze or interpret the papers or documents included there. The goal is to get students to actually dig around in the folder's contents and to make connections between what's there and what they've been learning about their writing, about academic discourse, or about the subject matter of their projects.

The following prompts are designed to make good, reflective use of the writing folder — to give students opportunities to improve the organization of their materials, but also, most important, to ask them to reflect on what they see in their folders, especially in terms of patterns or connections. In sorting through it all, reminding themselves what's there, and reordering pages in ways that make sense, students can make the working folder more than "busy work": They can make it an important part of their learning experience.

- Reorganize the working folder into a different order than project-by-project: Put all of the notes and planning together; put all of the discovery drafts together; put all of the peer response forms or letters together; put all of your "final" or edited drafts together. Now, what do you notice about each of these "sets"?

- With the working folder in any order, find patterns for each of the following:

    1. Topics or interests. Is there a "theme" or thread that runs through most of your projects?

    2. Writing processes or strategies. How did your steps or strategies differ for different assignments? Or do you always follow the same basic routine?

    3. Problems, struggles, or errors. What areas of writing do you find the hardest, and why? Can you identify areas in which you get stuck or feel frustrated? Does it happen with each project?

Cultivating the reflective learning habit through the working folder requires portfolio teachers to write effective prompts, guides, or questions, and it requires students to be responsible learners, organized and caught up. The working folder may be graded, near the end of the semester, for its "completeness" or lack thereof, or for the evidence it offers of students' willingness and ability to explore the writing process fully. For example, if a folder contains only two drafts for each project — one for the peer response group and one for me, without significant revision in between — that folder does not demonstrate a writer's willingness to take risks in adding, deleting, moving, or rearranging. Pieces written to engage with the working folder may also be graded, based on evidence of a writer's ability to reflect on the contents, organization, and patterns found in the working folder. Despite these suggestions for what might be graded, the next section makes a case for *not grading drafts*.

To grade or not to grade?

—6—
Ongoing Assessment/ Postponed Grades

Once students are into the routine of a writing course, the instructor's role shifts a bit from course designer and facilitator to reader and respondent. During the middle weeks of the term, when students are writing their essays, exploring the writing process, and learning about rhetoric, the most important job for the instructor is to respond to the writing, with feedback and guidance that anticipates the portfolio. Starting from the assumption that our responses to student writing are crucial, fundamental, and hugely formative in students' experiences with writing, in this chapter I argue for engaged response and rigorous assessment that is not dependent on grades.

*When is the right time for **assessment**?* Anytime. From the beginning. Regularly.

*When is the right time for **grades**?* Late, late, late in the course.

Student writers will benefit if we maintain important distinctions between assessment and grading even though the two overlap or have definite similarities. Granted, grades are one form of assessment, but portfolio teaching gets better results when grades on writing projects are postponed, deemphasized, and kept separate from other forms of assessment. Confusing the two, or relying too much on grading (at least for writing classes), undermines process teaching and reflective learning — or it sends confusing and contradictory messages to students about the instructor's expectations. Are they supposed to revise this B paper? If so, to what end?

All working writers receive evaluation of their work, and useful evaluation fuels the writing process. Evaluation of students' writing is a crucial part of the learning process, but it occurs in two main forms: summative and formative. *Summative* evaluation, of course, summarizes and signals the end of the process, while *formative* evaluation takes place throughout the process and is a type of instructive intervention that shapes or changes the project's development. This distinction is important for portfolio teaching, and portfolio practitioners have been making the case against premature grading for years. Peter Elbow and Pat Belanoff write that "portfolios permit us to avoid putting grades on individual papers, and thereby help us make the evaluations we do during the semester formative, not summative" (1997, 29–30).

Valid reasons for evaluating student writing are to guide them on their way through a writing-intensive course (Lindemann 1995, 219), to diagnose students' writing problems (that is, to find and name the prose's strengths and

↝ type of writing Style.

weaknesses), and to identify repeated errors or mistakes. But in none of these cases is grading suggested or required. In *A Rhetoric for Writing Teachers*, Erika Lindemann reminds us that

> grading . . . is a closed procedure. Once we assign a grade, we've judged the paper in ways that further revision can't change. Although comments may accompany the grade, most students interpret them not as "feedback" but as a justification for the judgment we've made. From the students' perspective a graded paper is "finished," and additional work won't change either the grade or their feelings about succeeding or failing. (1995, 220)

Lindemann goes on to stress, as I also want to, that "grades represent a necessary form of evaluation," but if used prematurely or to replace response, they can do more harm than good. Premature grades work against a process writing course; they can short-circuit students' development or discourage them from taking risks: "Grades undermine improvement in writing because they restrict and pervert students' naturally developing sense of audience awareness. Writing is its own heuristic; it doesn't have to be graded to lead to learning" (Elbow and Belanoff 1997, 30).

Assessment, like writing, is a process, and assessment better supports process-oriented learning. Assigning grades, on the other hand, is a product-centered act. Grades are certainly appropriate for pieces of writing at the end-of-the-process stage, but they are most productive if the piece is considered "finished," and if the grade will serve a clear purpose.

Grades serve mostly to satisfy the institution's and society's demands for ranking, while assessment helps students learn more about the complexities of writing. Assessment can and should go on throughout the learning period — in forms other than grading. Students conditioned by grades often focus on the evaluation of writing much more than on the process of writing, on what they learn by writing, or on the critical-thinking goals that our assignments try to build. It takes sustained or conscientious effort to move students' attention away from the grading and toward the writing/thinking process. One way to do this is to address the issue of grading head-on: to ask students about their experiences with grades on their writing, to share with them the difficulty of putting grades on written work, or to explain why certain types of assessments are more appropriate than others. Students will be interested in contrasting, for example, a multiple-choice exam in anatomy with an essay exam for history.

An obvious way to value assessment over grading, of course, is to resist grading several types of writing that students produce: (1) short writing-to-learn pieces or quick in-class responses; (2) pieces that have not yet been through a full round of reading, response, and revision; or (3) papers or writing projects that are not "finished." Each of these types of pieces, of course, can and should be assessed, but assessment can take many forms and often occurs when we may not even intend it. The following are ways of assessing student performance that have nothing to do with grades but that do serve to model reader behavior or readerly reactions to a text:

- Give a word of encouragement in class.
- Frown or smile while reading a paper quickly in conference.
- Offer very brief marginal comments: *Good point. Great line. What do you mean? Can you say more? Well-said. I'm confused. Any examples? Are you sure? I like this passage. Nice pace. The perfect word.*
- Insert one line at the end, an overall comment: *This gets better as it moves along.* Or: *Your second sentence is the strongest.* Or: *A little thin on support.* Or: *Do readers need so much summary?*
- Make use of codes and symbols. Any responding reader has a repertoire of codes and symbols — I use stars (for high praise), question marks, exclamation points, and maybe a rare smiley face. I try not to use correction symbols or to circle errors because for most of these informal pieces, it's not time for that kind of editing (and may never be), and my corrections only send contradictory messages about what's important. If I've let students know ahead of time that I will edit the sentences, I do so to show them what patterns of problems or errors they need to be aware of.
- Ask students to read, comment on, or assess one another's work, especially for journals or impromptu writing assignments.
- Ask students to assess their own work.

CHALLENGING STUDENTS' ASSUMPTIONS ABOUT ASSESSMENT

Students' attitudes about assessment have been shaped, of course, by their experiences in school, but some of their assumptions or expectations are not going to fit with ours. Even when we take great pains to connect our forms of evaluating student performance to our pedagogical practices and commitments, students might not see the connection. It's worth it, therefore, to spend a bit of class time addressing the stereotypes, assumptions, or notions that students bring with them into our classes, and to share with them our own theories of, approaches to, or goals for assessment. In *Portfolio Keeping* I list and discuss the following six myths of assessment and encourage students to discuss the implications of these myths. Prompted by the discussion of these myths in that guidebook, students may ask you what your position is on these myths or what others you would add.

Myth No. 1   Instructors love giving grades on written work; they find it easy to decide what the letter grade should be on any particular essay, story, or exam.

Myth No. 2   Instructors value only error-free prose. When they read, they look mostly at commas and spelling.

Myth No. 3   Instructors spend most of their free time correcting student papers.

Myth No. 4   A letter grade is the only or the best way to assess student performance in writing.

Myth No. 5   Instructors are autonomous, independent, and can do whatever they want.

Myth No. 6   The evaluation of writing is purely subjective, and everyone is entitled to his or her opinion.

You or your students may be able to add to this incomplete list of beliefs, unfounded or not, about grades, teachers as graders, and the relationship between grading and student work or attitudes. Discussions along these lines can help students understand the complexities of assessment, just as they may remind you of the legitimacy of students' complaints and frustrations. Students may not quite believe you, but it's worth trying to show them that you are a reader first and a teacher second, and that your first priority is not grading or wielding power but responding to their work in ways that help them to anticipate readers' needs.

Those new to or skeptical of the portfolio method might ask, "But without a grade, where's the student's motivation?" In my experience, students are hugely relieved and stimulated when they learn that they have weeks to practice and improve before the grade stakes are high. Just as a jazz band would practice for weeks before the spring concert, or a basketball team would practice for weeks before the season begins, writers need practice time, too, before the work goes public. Students' motivation comes from the opportunity and the responsibility that the portfolio method provides, because students get to decide the fate of their work.

The idea that grades are motivation came mostly from formerly good students who received good grades. (And many of them, hooked on the rewards of school, went on to become teachers.) In my experience, it's only the best students, those with a history of A's, who are uncomfortable without grades on drafts. Easygoing students not so dependent on grades, cynical students who know grades are a game, and eager students who like a challenge or change of pace seem quite content to work on their pieces without knowing the grade. In any case, students choose, for reasons we cannot know, whether to accept, resist, or negotiate among the roles our classes provide for them. As a teacher, I can only give them opportunities to learn and, with their effort, to succeed.

WAYS TO ASSESS

Of course, students want and deserve to know where they stand in relation to others, or how their work can be ranked or judged. This ranking will occur — but it will be postponed until the end of the course. For anxious students, I am always willing to meet about grades in conference, as long as they bring their working folders so that we can have a conversation about their learning that's a little more involved than "What grade am I getting?"

When students receive projects back from me, they find a graded post-write, with a few comments on it, and then a variety of written comments on the draft. Most of my *marginal* comments are in the form of questions or praise. My *end* comments — on the last page or on the back — begin, usually, with one sentence about the project's strengths or about what works well; they follow quite predictably the genre of the end comment (Smith 1997). The most important clause in my end comment is "If you revise." I try to emphasize to students their options and their responsibility in the portfolio process as well as the rhetorical lessons that I want them to be learning or the discourse features that the assignment emphasizes. Writing good end comments — those that students will read — requires enormous time and care, because if the comments are too predictable, students won't read them (Smith 1997, 268). While instructors usually try to be "facilitative" rather than "directive" in their responses, research by Richard Straub demonstrates that a combination of both can be effective or appropriate. Because, as Straub points out, "all teacher comments in some way are evaluative and directive," teachers need to develop different strategies for intervening in a student's writing process and must ask themselves critical questions about when and to what extent they should exert control over students' writing. Most important, teachers should, through their commentary, create themselves as readers (Straub 1996, 246–47).

Though I do not grade individual projects along the way, not even secretly on my spreadsheet, I do give grades for other parts of the process. For example, the postwrite that accompanies each project is graded; a peer response form included with the project may be graded; and if the project has been written collaboratively, each student's participation or contribution may be graded — but the draft itself does not receive a grade.

Plenty of assessment, in different forms, will guide students as they begin to make the choices leading to their portfolios — choices that take center stage near the end of the course, when it's time to make informed decisions, revise the material, and then present a quality portfolio.

PART TWO

THE CULMINATION OF THE COURSE

—7—

The Time-to-Decide Conference

Near the end of the course, with approximately two or three weeks remaining, practice time gives over to performance time, and the portfolio begins to come together. With an introduction to the portfolio on the first day, attention to the working folder, and plenty of opportunities for reflective learning, students are ready to make choices, revise, and present their work. So with two or three weeks left in the course, it's time to give students some specific instructions about the portfolio — your expectations, guidelines, or advice — and to get them started on an intensive period of choosing and revising, and reflecting on those choices and changes.

I reserve a full class period for reviewing and discussing what's going to happen in the remaining weeks or class sessions. I give each student a two-page handout titled "Time to Decide," the contents of which are shared in this section. At the end of this class discussion, students sign up for their group conferences and begin reviewing their working folders. Throughout this class and the conferences, I try to emphasize the connection between making choices and showing students what they've learned. If everything could be included, for example, where does the learning kick in? If portfolios were all-inclusive, which they are not, how would students apply what they have learned about purpose and audience and tailoring prose to meet the needs of readers? The work of the course starts here!

Giving students some structure and guidance for choosing their portfolio entries certainly does not have to take place in a conference, but I have found it valuable. Still, when it comes time to decide, when the moment has arrived to select the entries and to begin revising them, students do need some help and should have many questions.

Because the portfolio method is new for many of my students, and because I find conferencing valuable anyway, I schedule "time-to-decide" conferences with students, either individually or in groups or a combination of both. (I am fortunate that my writing program supports the idea of replacing one or two class meetings, once or twice a semester, with conferences.) This time-to-decide conference is scheduled with about two weeks of classes remaining, or about three weeks left in the term, and its purpose is made clear by its title: It's time for students to decide which projects they want to pursue for inclusion in their final portfolio. They don't need to make every decision at this point, but they do need to commit to revising one or two projects and to begin planning how their final portfolio will look in terms of its contents, organization, and presentation.

The heart of this stage is the working folder. I suggest that students find a large table and spread out the contents of their working folders (with everything labeled, dated, or otherwise organized and accessible). Many students have no trouble making most of the decisions, at least when some structure is provided. For example, if three portfolio entries are required, most students can choose two of those fairly quickly. Here are the types of questions that help students to decide which pieces to include in the portfolio; they are my way of "intervening" in the process without voting directly on what students should include. These are not the only possibilities for shaping the portfolio, but one of these may trigger an idea or help to get the process started.

- Do you want to show progress — that is, how much your writing and thinking has improved?
- Do you want to show steadfastness, your ability to stick with a project for a long period?
- Do you want to show your flexibility, that you can write in different styles or voices?
- Do you want to show creativity, or how you have made the assignments your own?
- Do you want to show independence, that you have revised well beyond the suggestions, or made considerably more changes than were recommended?

Students will naturally want to select those pieces that their readers have thought "the best," or those they most enjoyed writing. They may appreciate, however, having other options: They could choose a paper to include that shows considerable promise or potential. It may still need quite a bit of work to prepare it for the final presentation, but students would be able to talk about doing that work in the reflective introduction. Being able to demonstrate an understanding of revision through a smartly revised paper could be just as satisfying as including one already considered "the best."

PRECONFERENCE PLANNING

I ask students to prepare in specific ways for the time-to-decide conference. In a class on the day that we schedule conferences, we discuss the portfolio guidelines, requirements, expectations, or options, taking as much time as we need. Then I ask students to review, organize, and label the contents of their working folders in any way that might be useful to them during the decision and revision process.

I encourage students to use their own instincts and reactions to pieces to judge whether they should be submitted. If they can't get excited about a piece, how will they make readers like it? Boredom shows, so they should choose pieces for which they still have energy, enthusiasm, or ideas for revision.

Questions to Ask Students about Choosing the Entries

Here are some questions that should encourage students to consider the possibilities in selecting their portfolio entries.

- Which piece could you start working on right now, knowing you could make it better?
- Which one do you have the most energy for revisiting?
- What pieces do you just feel good about? Which ones went well in the process?
- What essays do you think your response group liked best?
- To which pieces did your readers respond most positively or enthusiastically?
- In which paper do your strengths really shine?
- Which one surprised you?
- Which topic made you want to find more information or do some research?
- Which piece did you work really hard on, and what's your definition of working hard on a piece of writing?
- Which one wasn't going well but somehow turned out pretty well?
- Which paper was the hardest or longest piece you've ever written, one you're quite proud of?

On the other hand, here are a few questions for eliminating possibilities, which most students find easy enough to do:

- Which essay would you just dread working on again? You look at it and read the comments and can't think of one thing more you have to say.
- As you begin rereading it, do changes occur to you?

- Do you have the energy to revisit this paper, even if you don't have specific ideas for revision? Can you get a little excited about having another shot at it?

The questions or prompts may vary considerably from these, but the bottom line is to provide guidance for those students who want it, and to make sure that they have energy and ideas for revising a portfolio piece.

CONFERENCING

Because ten-minute conferences with each of sixty students (for example) would require ten hours — a schedule very few writing teachers can manage (even with canceled class meetings) — I find group conferences to be a good alternative. As my office doesn't hold five people (whose does?), I meet with students either in our classroom, in small seminar rooms in the library, or in the quietest corners of a cafeteria at off times of day. Then, for those students who seem to be struggling or need more attention, a few individual conferences can also happen during my regular office hours.

If students come prepared in directed ways, it is possible to accomplish quite a bit in a twenty- or thirty-minute meeting even though it may feel rushed. (If you have sixty students and they come in groups of four, twenty-minute meetings require five hours). Students *must* bring their working folders, prefaced by a table of contents, and I ask for a revision plan for the portfolio entry about which they are most excited or sure. Before this meeting, then, students need to spend time organizing and updating their folders, if they have fallen behind, or reviewing the contents of their working folders thoroughly enough to know at least one of the entries they want to include in the portfolio. They may "commit" to only one entry or several, but they should remain open-minded, for the conference, about some of their entries — so that they can listen to and learn from other students' choices and rationales. Students should bring to the conference

- their working folders, organized, updated, labeled, and reviewed;
- questions about anything they're unsure of;
- a firm revision plan for at least one entry they would like to include; and
- possible other entries, with ideas about each.

Options, choices, and rationales become the focus of the time-to-decide conference. Each student is responsible for presenting, very briefly, the choices he or she has already made and why, and what choices remain. In addition, students need to have two or three questions — for the group — about their portfolio plans or ideas, and a revision plan for one of their projected entries. Because it is not possible for individuals to read full drafts aloud or share all of one essay, revisions or new versions are not a priority. We begin with general questions and then move to three-minute reports from each student, which usually expand into a discussion that quickly fills the time slot.

To emphasize choices and responsibility, I will *not* tell or advise students what to include in their portfolios. The preceding questions are my way of intervening, but I try to encourage students to make their own decisions, based on their "gut feeling" about a paper, the responses they've received from me and from their peers, and the ideas they have about revising. If they just don't want to revisit a particular assignment or project, then they shouldn't.

—8—
Assigning the Reflective Introduction

Students who have maintained a working folder and have managed to save, label, and file all of their paperwork for this class can now be grateful and can reap the benefit of their organizational skills. If they have kept track of their writing processes for each assignment and their struggles and successes, they can use much of this collected information to write their portfolio's reflective introduction, cover letter, self-assessment piece, or the description that prefaces each of the entries. This piece, if it does come first, could be the most important text students will write all semester because it will show their ability to be a reflective learner and to analyze and respond to the rhetorical situation effectively. In many ways, students' reflective introductions (or conclusions, if you'd rather the reflective piece be at the end) are the "final exam" for the course. This piece, wherever it's placed, brings together students' understanding of both of the situations involved with a portfolio writing course — the keeping part and the assessment part. The keeping in which students have been engaged now evolves into rhetorically informed choices.

CONSIDERATIONS IN ASSIGNING
THE REFLECTIVE ELEMENT

The reflective portion of the portfolio will be more developed or more thoughtful if instructors spend a considerable amount of time in class reviewing and discussing its role in the portfolio. If you have prepared for or anticipated all the possibilities, students will be clearer about the expectations.

- Should the reflective piece come first in the portfolio — often called a cover letter or an introduction — or can it appear elsewhere? Do I really want it to be a "letter," addressed to me, or might it be written in the more traditional essay form?

- Should I ask for reflection before or after each entry instead? Or should I have students include a piece at the end that serves as a conclusion or postscript?
- Should I ask for a reflective element to the portfolio but let individual students make the decisions about what that is, where it goes, and why it goes there?
- How much information should I give students about the reflective parts to their portfolio? How much coaching or how extensive the modeling?
- If the piece is to be an introductory *letter,* should I ask for business letter format, with, for example, inside addresses, block style, and a proper salutation?

After exploring the implications of each of these decisions, you'll be ready to present this assignment to students. In addition, if you have introduced the reflective piece through first-week orientation to the class, and if you have reminded students periodically throughout the semester that the postwrites and other "reflective" assignments are giving them practice, then they are prepared to write this assignment. With about two or three weeks left in the term, schedule thirty to forty-five minutes of a class period to preview this assignment with students, to discuss their options and to clarify its purpose and importance. Part of the handout I distribute to students to help them with this assignment appears on page 44.

As you present and explain this important assignment to your students, the following questions or discussion topics can highlight the rhetorical nature of this assignment:

- Who will be reading this piece? Is the reader reading to suggest changes or reading it to evaluate your work and make a decision about your effort and talent?
- What is the situation surrounding this reading?
- What will the outcome of the reading be, and how much can you influence the outcome?
- What qualities of writing will your reader value?

Even a simple question such as "How long should it be?" can trigger a good conversation about the relationship between length and quality, or the importance of development (examples and the like) without "padding" the writing. Students will also be interested in talking about their own experiences with first impressions, if the reflective portion comes first, and will be able to identify good and bad decisions that may affect the "first impression" factor.

For example, ask students to brainstorm what would be inappropriate claims to make in their reflective introductions to a portfolio worth a large percentage of the course grade. In other words, what would be just really dumb things to say? What kinds of statements or claims would be unwise, ill-considered, or at least risky? (My students often respond with "To say you haven't learned anything" or "To admit your writing isn't any better" or "If the paper is full of errors.") This discussion usually moves into whether they should "ask for an A" or whether flattering the reader is appropriate. Be prepared for the student who claims he will ask for an A because he can prove that he deserves one. You may want to consider ahead of time what your rhetorically informed response will be or how you will discuss this strategy with students, who have a right to know if you will react strongly to such an appeal. If you know from experience that you "hate it" when students do that, it's only fair to tell them what your own recognized idiosyncrasies are as an evaluator.

More important, though, is to get students to see the rhetorical layers behind such a bold request for a certain course grade and how such a request (or demand) might be presented in ways that fit with the expectation for reflection or self-assessment. If, for example, a student can support his request for an A by referring to the course policies and grading criteria, or by paraphrasing and quoting extensively from his working folder, I would be much more open to such a passage in the reflective introduction.

Similarly, portfolio teachers need to anticipate obvious attempts at flattery or teacher pleasing, which some students may choose as a rhetorical strategy. I discuss "schmoozing" later in this chapter, but if teachers know it will be a turn-off, they should announce that to students. I suggest to my students that flattery runs the risk of underestimating my sophistication as a reader or my years of experience with reading student texts. Having been reminded that you've "seen it all before," students might be hard-pressed to come up with more original forms of flattery, or they might have to make their case differently.

MODELING REFLECTIVE INTRODUCTIONS: PROS AND CONS

Because using imitation to teach rhetoric predates Plato, teachers' natural inclination is to give students models for effective reflective pieces. The instinct is a sound one: If we're emphasizing the importance of this piece of writing to students' success in the course, then shouldn't we show them good ones? If a variety of good ones are shared or made available, a case can be made for their use, but each teacher should weigh the benefits and disadvantages of sharing models. Because writing the reflective portion is often the equivalent of a final exam, or a test of what students have learned about qualities of good writing, anticipating readers' needs, and the importance of careful self-presentation, you might decide that students need to create their reflective essays without models or samples. On the other hand, if this piece *is* crucial to students' success with this assignment and the portfolio, and models could help them to succeed, then why not provide some? One concern is that students will sidestep their own decision-making or creative choices the reflective introduction, you might try some of the following (but you can't choose all of these options):

- Discuss your best entry and why it is your best.
- Detail the revisions you've made and the improvements and changes that you want readers to notice.
- Discuss each piece of writing included, touching on the strengths of each.
- Outline the process that one or more of your entries went through.
- Demonstrate what this portfolio illustrates about you as a writer, student, researcher, or critical thinker.
- Acknowledge your weaknesses but show how you've worked to overcome them.
- Acknowledge the reader-respondents who have influenced your portfolio pieces and how.
- Reflect on what you've learned about writing, reading, or other topics of the course.
- Prepare your reader for a positive evaluation of your work.

You have many options in writing an effective introduction — there is no magic formula or model text — but you will need to demonstrate self-assessment; in other words, show that you can evaluate the strengths of your work, that you understand what you do well and what you still need to work on.

The reflective introduction is also the place where both process and product come together. Readers of your portfolio have not been able to see your process. They haven't watched you write, haven't participated in your peer response groups, haven't seen all of your notes, drafts, and other evidence of your evolving ideas. They won't know what your friend suggested about the anecdote that opens your argument essay, and they won't know how hard you've worked on adding transitions between paragraphs. Readers will be aware only of what you share with them in the reflective piece.

and do the same things they see in a good model. Following a certa
or structure is common in professional writing, however; it show
understanding of rhetorical conventions. As long as samples from a range of
writers are shared or made available, sharing models can be a useful lesson.
The key to discouraging sameness is to give students several samples that
incorporate a variety of approaches, and to illustrate all the ways in which a
reflective piece can be successful.

TEACHING IDEAS FOR THE
REFLECTION ASSIGNMENT

A good reflection assignment should ask students to read critically, analyze
data, and see patterns. This list of assignments or activities, while not com-
prehensive, will help students practice reflection before the portfolio is due.

1. Have students analyze three different audiences for the reflective letter: (1) the classroom instructor, (2) instructors in the same program
   but unknown, and (3) classmates or peers. Students should decide
   which logical, ethical, or emotional appeals might be most effective for
   each audience, and what tone, language, or vocabulary would be
   appropriate for each. How do they know? What makes them think so?

2. If the college writing program has a set of guidelines or policies and
   grading criteria — in brochure form or on a Web page — ask students
   to consult it and to come to a consensus about what information they
   can use for their reflective introductions.

3. Ask students to look back through their working folders and to cate-
   gorize or classify the instructor's comments on their returned papers.
   At the same time, they should review the course syllabus and assignment
   sheets. What patterns do they see in their instructor's concerns or
   directions?

4. Ask students to imagine that a friend has asked if she should enroll in
   their instructor's section of writing or composition. What information
   would they give their friend about their instructor's expectations — or
   pet peeves? Students should call upon what they've learned about their
   instructor's values as a reader to compose a convincing, well-developed
   reflective letter.

5. Share several models of reflective introductions (from a previous class
   or colleagues' classes), and ask students to analyze them for effective-
   ness, strategies, appropriateness, and areas for improvement.

—9—
Reading and Grading the Portfolio

Formative evaluation is an important part of portfolio courses — that is, it is an ongoing assessment of students' performance in a variety of forms. After consistent and routine formative evaluation, however, **summative evaluation** becomes necessary. For most of us, that means assigning letter grades at the end of the course. In my classes, the portfolio is worth between 40 percent or 50 percent of the final course grade. (The other 50 to 60 percent is assigned to graded postwrites; peer response forms; journals, reading-response papers, or other short, informal writings; writing folder checkups; participation or "good citizenship"; or a final exam.) Grades on final portfolios are determined the old-fashioned way: by reading what's included and deciding on each portfolio's ranking.

Although each writing instructor needs to develop his or her own routine, mechanism, or rubrics for grading student work — a process aided by years of experience and conversations with other teachers, as well as by the literature on grading — the portfolio should receive a single grade even if there are several entries included. The term for this from the assessment literature is *holistic evaluation* — judging the portfolio as a whole, with the full weight of first impressions. When it's time to *grade* the portfolio, *commenting* or *responding* is **not** your job. The opportunity to intervene has passed by. Summative evaluation remains an important part of instruction. I will circle or otherwise mark errors and mistakes and record such familiar symbols as stars, question marks, or exclamation marks, but I don't write comments any longer than brief phrases: *Catchy title; This is powerful; Great example; Any evidence?; I'm confused; Super sentences here.* Responding is optional because you have already done the difficult and time-consuming work of guiding students' revisions. Since that stage has been completed, and the portfolio marks the end of the practice period, grading the portfolio with nothing more than a letter grade — no marks, notes, or questions — is perfectly appropriate, as long as students understand this or know what to expect. Putting only a grade and no comments is not only pedagogically sound in this situation but is also a straightforward time-management issue. As I discuss later about managing the paper load, portfolios needn't be a burden at the end of a semester.

Students can develop a keen understanding of the grading situation if they are invited to develop the rubric or "grading criteria" for the assessment. In an English methods course, for example, C. Beth Burch worked with her students to agree on certain criteria for the portfolio, including "organization, originality and creativity, variety, pedagogical soundness, practicality, and evidence of effort" (1997, 264). When the group could not reach consensus on weighting the criteria, "I left that task up to each student. The result was a rubric allowing adjustments for individual strengths and weaknesses" (264). In developing any scoring guide, the trick is to match what the assignment asks for with what the criteria require. For a portfolio in a first-year composition course, we want to see evidence that students understand the rhetorical situation of assessment, that can articulate reasons for their choices and the revision processes that went into the portfolio, and so forth. A scoring guide should describe features of, roughly, a *superior* response to the assignment, a *strong* response, a *competent* response, a *weak* response, an *inadequate* response, and an *incompetent* response. These terms, of course, can vary, and there can be more than six levels, but this model has evolved from large-scale writing assessments such as those designed by the Educational Testing Service.

In developing a rubric, some of the following questions may come up, and each is worth considering in some detail.

- **How much revision is enough?** This should be determined in consultation with the student or through general expectations distributed to students or discussed in class — well before the portfolio is submitted. In other words, grading the final portfolio is not the time to determine if "enough" revision has occurred; grading the final portfolio means that the question has already been answered. The act of submitting the final portfolio indicates that the writing process, including adequate revision, has been completed, given the time limits and other constraints of a composition course. The precise amount or type of revision is not "visible" in the final portfolio although it may be discussed explicitly in the reflective introduction. Because the portfolios I collect contain only clean, final copies, without drafts, the introduction or a preface to each entry clarifies the most important changes made to the entries. Otherwise, the proof of revising and editing is in the pudding; they cannot be treated as isolated variables in the assessment of the whole package.

- **How much should "the process" count?** Because every person's writing process differs for each and every writing task, grading a writer's process is a very tricky and problematic practice — especially in the age of word processing. Should those students with careful outlines, messy drafts, pages of clustering, or dozens of note cards receive more points than students without? Are we sure that a careful outline or a messy draft is really leading toward a better piece of writing? It's tempting to grade evidence of students' processes because we want students to become familiar enough with the steps and stages to apply the writing process to other writing situations. We also need to discourage plagiarism as well as last-minute writing. Writers make so many changes onscreen, however, that it's impossible to track or record most of the changes made in an evolving draft. In the temptation to grade the notes or the number of drafts, we may forget that it's the product that really counts. For classroom portfolios graded at the end of a term, the product contains the writing process or embodies the process; therefore, teachers can and should grade the portfolio as a final product with a single grade. The time to "grade the process" occurs throughout the course: Each time I grade postwrites I am assessing students' sense of the writing process and their strategies or repertoire for negotiating particular assignments. Instructors can also grade working folders not only for how complete or organized they are, but also for how well they demonstrate the steps a writer has taken in working her way through a rhetorical task.

- **How much should improvement count?** After students have been with us for several weeks, it's difficult not to have an instinctive sense of their improvement, but can we really measure improvement? It is tempting to compare the portfolio version of a paper to an earlier one and look for improvements or actual evidence of revision. Because the portfolio includes only clean, final copies and not the entire working folder, however, that temptation has to be replaced by fresh readings, by a sense of the whole package. Not having the earlier versions increases the chances that we will evaluate the portfolio for what it is — for the actual product and for how it meets or doesn't meet the goals and expectations of the course. I do, of course, find myself comparing, sometimes, the portfolio version of a paper with an earlier draft. I have a good memory for students' papers and cannot block out what I know about the evolution of an essay. But the test of the portfolio is not how an individual paper has changed or improved (or hasn't). I am careful to review with students the fact that I will not have the drafts or earlier versions to serve as comparisons. Because my reading will be fresh and uninfluenced by earlier versions in the same folder, students may be less likely to make only those changes I suggested. Of course, I may recognize changes or realize that a student hasn't made any, but I do not intentionally set out to compare versions. And as we know, revising is not an automatic improvement — revising does not guarantee a "better" essay, just a different one. In addition, reading to determine a grade is about more than "Is this version better than the last one I saw?" You have to consider the status or quality of the package of writings as a whole.

- **How do we account for the choices or the variety?** How can evaluators call one portfolio markedly better than another when they may contain different types of writing? If all of the portfolios in a given class contain a different combination of final entries, how can they be compared with or ranked against one another? This is yet another argument for a class-developed rubric, with students having both input and insight into the evaluation process. In addition, it helps to have a broader notion of variety than just "different genres." Variety also means pieces written at different "moments" and for different audiences, or composed with different aims or purposes. In the context of most first-year composition courses, variety does not mean a wide variety of genres or types of writing; it results from other factors.

- **Then what are we looking for, exactly?** What factors should be taken into account? The preceding paragraphs above warn evaluators against comparing portfolio entries to earlier versions and against looking only for evidence of revision or improvement. In grading the final portfolio, however, **we need to assess how well students negotiate the complexity of this rhetorical situation** and assess the overall quality of their writing. What evidence do you find of students' understanding of the rhetorical situation the portfolio presents? What choices have they made about content and arrangement, and how effective is their sense of audience? What choices have they made about self-presentation, and how do they represent themselves as readers, writers, and learners? Where do you see good habits paying off? Where do you find proof of effort, responsibility, or revision? As I will try to illustrate, *what students say about their work* in a reflective introduction or essay constitutes much of what evaluators need to determine a grade or ranking.

GETTING THE GRADING DONE

Here's my own grading process: I try to set aside a big chunk of uninterrupted time to complete the reading and grading for one class. (Interrupted time — for example, grading half of the papers one day and the other half three days later — means that I lose my sense of the class as a whole.) I get comfortable as I would for reading a novel or doing something I expect to enjoy. (I don't sit at a table or desk as I do for responding extensively to papers.) I sit on the couch with pillows and with my feet up. I have a pencil in my hand for marking errors, and for recording notes that communicate my reading response — for recording question or exclamation marks, smiley faces, or one- or two-word responses like "Good details" and "Very convincing" and "Why?"

From my comfortable spot, I read through the whole set quickly but completely — making all of the markings or comments that I am likely to make — giving each portfolio a tentative grade in pencil and placing each portfolio into one of three stacks: high range, medium range, and low range. Then I go through each stack separately, sorting more specifically the high-range, medium-range, and low-range portfolios. Once that is done, I confirm or change my pencil grade accordingly. Each portfolio grade is determined within the context of the whole set, and each grade reflects the class standard. That doesn't mean that the "best" portfolio necessarily gets an A (often it's an A- or occasionally even a B+), but sorting and ranking them helps me distinguish the B- from the C+.

What I can't account for or explain are the actual cognitive processes that lead me to say, "This is a B, and *this* isn't." What we do know from some research on evaluating portfolios is that the cover letter, reflective introduction, or first few pages make the most significant impression of any other portfolio entry (Conway 1994; Hamp-Lyons and Condon 1993; Black 1994). My own experiences or intuitions fit with this research. The reflective introductions do seem to figure largely in my evaluation of a portfolio — mostly because of what students say about their work. In fact, I believe that *what students say about their own work* gives us plenty to go on in determining a fair grade.

In this next section, I want to quote passages from some of my students' reflective introductions, written for two sections of Writing 101 and one section of Writing 301 in the fall of 1998. My purpose in sharing these is not necessarily to provide "models" but to illustrate the kinds of passages that particularly struck me in my reading and grading process — passages that I really needed to pay attention to or think about. Although my categories for interpreting these "acts of reflection" in portfolio introductions may be representative, the actual samples or passages will differ in every portfolio writing class. Students' claims, examples, and approaches to this assignment will grow out of the context of the course (as they should). Teachers preparing to read and grade their own students' portfolios, however, might benefit from seeing how one instructor responded. In general, I am trying to be reflective about how I read and grade these portfolios.

Because this assignment was quite specific about demonstrating reflection, I share samples of student writing that accomplish this. I've also quoted passages that show other types of understanding about the class or about writing; another set of passages illustrates typical patterns I see in these reflective introductions (sometimes, despite my best efforts). Following several passages of student writing is a discussion of "glow and schmooze," an effect that many portfolio readers have noticed.

Evidence of the Ability to Be Reflective

When we say we want students to reflect on their learning, on their writing processes, or on their choices, what exactly do we mean? The following passages demonstrate lessons learned, discoveries made, or realizations achieved.

> I have learned how to organize myself for a writing task by jotting down ideas, making lists of important points, writing rough half-thoughts when they come to mind and how to incorporate all of this into a piece of writing. Learning to write then put it away and come back to it later has become a very useful tool in my writing process. This course has shown me that it's O.K. to scrap ideas, even good ones, if they are not relevant to the subject at hand. — *Amy*

It has taken me a while, but I'm more capable of fixing the problems in my writing. I am getting better at recognizing when I wander off from the focus of the paper. Also, I am learning how much information to give, what's too little and what's too much. I know that I have to seriously consider my audience before I start writing. I have to figure out how much they might know and how much they might not know. I also have to figure out how to make a certain kind of audience interested in a specific topic; I need to know what would make them angry, upset, or pleased. — *Carol*

The second entry weaves together quotations from all five postwrites. I analyzed what I had written in each one and what I had learned and I discovered that through the postwrites I had grown tremendously over the course of the semester. In the first three postwrites I didn't know where my paper was headed. About halfway through the semester I realized that by not freewriting or brainstorming or making an outline, I was having a difficult time focusing. That slowly began to change as I began to understand how to focus my papers. By writing the postwrites after writing each paper, I learned to analyze my work so that I could revise. — *Sharon*

As a writer, I feel that I have learned how to take criticism and work with it to improve my opinion of my papers. I have also learned more efficient and up-to-date options for research. In addition, I was able to encounter new ways of brainstorming ideas and new techniques for organizing my pieces. — *Rebecca*

On Revision

It's important to note here that reflection means revision, too. A writer cannot make many changes in a paper or make decisions about its purpose or organization or tone without being reflective. So when reflective introductions discuss the writer's revision processes explicitly, the reader/evaluator gets a double dose of reflection.

In revising [the review of <u>The Neverending Story</u>], I took a couple of lines from the original introduction, copied them down onto another piece of paper, added a few more sentences, and rewrote the rest of the original piece. . . . I kept most of the description, and a couple of the opinions, but my final copy took on a whole new face. Instead of bashing the movies, like I did in the first review, I tried to concentrate on recommending the book. I wanted to give my review a more positive light. The original review was too negative. I had created the impression that the movies were to be avoided at all costs, which was not what I intended to do. Instead, I simply wanted to praise the book, make readers aware that there is a book, and still keep the movies in good standing. — *Carol*

My writing has been transformed through the past fourteen weeks. Not only have I made improvements and learned valuable techniques, but I am also able to identify the strong and weak aspects of my writing. This allows me to expand upon the strong points and fix the weak ones, thus making my writing better. Through the many workshops and revisions that we have done for this class, I now see the importance of revision and its effects. I am able to read my own work critically and revise areas of weakness myself. Revision would probably be one of the most important lessons I have learned about writing in this class. — *Kristin*

Overall, my weakness was organization. It is a flaw I have endeavored to correct, and I feel that I have finally done so. Through revision I have changed paragraphs, moved, chopped, dropped, added, and altered whole sections to make the paper "fit" together right. I believe that I have accomplished my goal. — *Nathalie*

Our project was originally directed toward a fictitious publishing company. However, I always had my father in mind. He became my audience when I began revising this piece for the portfolio because he is the one who I hope can really take this trip someday. With that in mind, the project became much more gratifying and enjoyable to complete. I felt as if the piece was fulfilling more than one purpose. It became a portfolio piece and my father's dream. When the audience changed, the criteria changed. . . . [My father] would not be interested in reading about the customs of the food because he was born and bred there. He would want to know where he is going, how to get there, and what to expect when he arrived at each destination. Taking in these considerations, the piece worked out very well, presenting everything my father was looking for in his traveling package. In the end, this project ended up being my favorite assignment. — *Karina*

Choices and Why

My assignment sheet for the reflective introduction specifically asks students to identify some of the choices they made and why. It sounds simple enough, but some students have more success with this than do others, and I think some students believe it's too obvious to spend much time on, or they can't say much beyond "I liked these the best" or "I spent the most time on these."

I elected these three papers because they each possess traits of a style of writing that I enjoy publishing. I feel that all required a good deal of ingenuity, descriptiveness, and persuasiveness to appeal to the reader. These are namely the qualities that have captivated me to thoroughly enjoy writing. — *Jesse*

My first paper illustrates my opinion on the portrayal of cities on TV. I tried to match the style of the piece with the thesis. For example, the paragraphs are cut off abruptly. It is meant to deliver a hammering and relentless feel, analogous to the quick button pushing of the remote control, and that's how I end the paper, too. I feel that this was creative. — *Nathalie*

> What I have chosen to do with this portfolio is a bit different than the suggestions given, but it is also the best way for me to show the process that I have gone through. The thing that is different is that I have chosen to include not only my best work, but also my work that is definitely my poorest. I feel that college is about the student's growth and development. For this reason I have included my best projects as well as my worst. — *Bryan*

Evidence of Rhetorical Savvy

These passages tell me that these writers really understand the reader/writer relationship and know something about how to cultivate it.

> When I write a paper, I write it in hopes that it will have an effect on the reader in some way. It doesn't matter if the reader only thinks about my paper for five minutes after they read it, or remembers it five years down the road. As long as it had some kind of impact on the reader, then I have met my goal. I specifically chose these three papers, to include in my portfolio, because I feel they have the qualities to meet my writing goal. — *Jennifer*

> The first paper deviates from the other three in that its focus is on me, the author. It's not so much an "issues" paper as it is a personal anecdote, and though this genre is not my particular favorite, I included it to give the reader a more intimate look at the author. Readers tend to respond more warmly to papers if they trust the author, and trust comes with familiarity. — *Tom*

Acknowledging Peer Respondents

Students did use some good rhetorical strategies in appealing to what they knew I would find valuable; for example, some credited their peer respondents for a lot of help.

In closing, I would like to note that the work contained in this portfolio would not have been improved without the help of you, Dr. Reynolds, and two special students, Jenn and Abigail. Jenn, Abby, and I worked together in every writing workshop and also helped each other outside of class. The three of you served as my critics, supporters, and creative thinkers. You are all true "wordsmiths" and I hope to carry the lessons you taught me into every piece I write in the future. — *Julie*

The Five-Paragraph Theme

A number of introductions found students falling back on the tried-and-true five-paragraph theme, even though, of course, that was never a focus of our course.

This is an introduction to my final portfolio. My final portfolio will include project three, a commentary titled "Tattoos Are Not That Bad"; project one, a literacy narrative titled "Keep In Touch"; and project five, a review titled "A Review of Misery." — *Newton*

This portfolio is a representation of the progress I have made this semester. I have chosen to include three pieces of my work. The first piece will be a combination of the two self-assessments we wrote in class, now titled "Learning to Write." The second one will be the paper on malls. My fifth project about confidence is the third selection. Through these pieces, I will show how my writing has improved. — *Amanda*

Frustrated by the dominance of this predictable structure when I tell students it's only appropriate for one- or two-hour timed writings, I should have seen earlier that it's a result of students feeling insecure or frustrated. Not knowing what the teacher wants, they fall back on the safety of a predictable package, on what has worked for them in the past.

"Creative" Approaches

Portfolio reader/evaluators will need to be prepared, if they invite creativity, to receive it. It may be worth thinking ahead about what it is you mean by "be creative," or what types of writing might "go too far." I have received passages that resist the assignment as they also attempt to do something different, like the following:

It's driving a straight road late into the night, the windows down and the heater up, the radio loud, but not too loud and it feels like you could just go on forever.

It's walking on a beach after sundown, late in the summer when you need a sweatshirt but can still walk barefoot along the shore, shoulder to shoulder and smile to smile with somebody you know you could stay with forever.

And it's standing in a crowded bar, drink in hand and friends in tow and a hundred people you've never seen and will never see again all lost, because you're lost in that someone you just met, and you wish the night would never end.

Only it does end. It doesn't go on forever. Soon enough we get busy with our lives. We have priorities and obligations and responsibilities. And fears. So we wait for the next moment, telling ourselves that this one won't get away.

This is, more than anything else, what I want to capture. . . . And maybe, if I can get it just right, maybe I can wrap my words around these times, around forever, and hold on tight.

For me, the words themselves always came easily. That was never the problem. The problem was the idea. I got lost in the words, sitting alone in front of a blank screen, a blank page. I babble on. I delete everything. So I try to be simpler. As simple as a walk on the beach. And as simple as a long romantic look.

Still it seems that we can be so afraid to take a chance. Those moments sit right in front of us, yet instead of reaching out to grab hold we too often push away. I want us to stop pushing. . . . I decided some time back that I could handle anything — except regret.

I hope that my writing will reflect this. — *Craig*

Dear Reader,

Have you ever walked along a quiet beach, your bare feet making impressions as you go? Often you become so engrossed in your thoughts that when you look back you are astounded at how far you have traveled. Your footprints create a wobbly pattern across the shoreline. You can stand and watch the tide erase parts of this trail, its metronomic arm unceasing in its devotion to the straightening of the sand. Looking back is a satisfying ritual. Today, dear reader, I invite you to join me in a metaphoric walk along my beach.

I have put together a cross-section of my work for you to sample. Each piece reflects my ability to write in a different style. After a brief self-assessment to introduce me as a writer, I have chosen four pieces I think exhibit my best work. The first two selections are reading response papers. One is about a book I enjoyed and the other I did not enjoy but I did appreciate. I wanted to show how I can be critical without being derogatory. Hopefully you will easily recognize which way my feelings leaned.

Next, I will sweep you off to paradise, but don't be too surprised if Eden has a few serpents. I am possessed of a satirical wit and have allowed it free rein in my tale, "Picture Perfect Travel." Lest you burn under the blazing sun, I promise to cool you down in a rainstorm. This piece, "Storm Warnings," has not one bit of humor in it. I purposely avoided by preferred style to exhibit my flexibility in writing. It is quite riveting, from my biased perspective.

While you are wringing out your bookmark, you can peruse my final analysis in which I briefly touch on how I have grown and changed as an author through this class. (I know it's a bit Freudian to be so analytical but I was a psychology major for many years and old habits die hard.)

I guess you are ready to proceed. Thank you for giving me a truly beneficial experience as a student. I know when you walk alone on the beach . . . you look back too. — *Alison*

While neither of these introductions explains choices very thoroughly, or introduces the contents or even reflects on the writer's learning, can I call such introductions unsuccessful? I found myself impressed, even if I did also find myself wishing for "more," perhaps, of what I expected or suggested or asked for. Instructors should let students know how much "room" they have in the introductions to play with conventions, be creative, or "have a voice."

Some of the entries I've just shared, I'm well aware, will be read or interpreted very differently by teachers or readers who don't "know" the students. I did draw these examples from the portfolios of students in my own classes, and context means everything. In fact, the question of context and interpretation leads into a messy area of portfolio evaluation that Irwin Weiser calls "glow and schmooze." "Glow" refers to the portfolio that starts out with a terrific introduction, meeting all of our expectations for a reflective preface, but then diminishes in quality. The writer succeeds at self-reflection and at explaining choices, but has not succeeded in putting together a strong package overall. "Schmooze" refers to those portfolio introductions that attempt to charm us or flatter us. While both features are subject to interpretation and "misreadings," I think Weiser has identified two difficult areas of assessing classroom portfolios. How should we grade portfolios that "fall apart" after the introduction? How do we (or should we) respond to passages in which students are thanking us for such a great class, marveling at how much they've learned, or claiming profound improvements in their writing? Some teachers worry about distinguishing between reflection and either appreciation or self-promotion. How do we know students are "sincere" in their introductory pieces when they make claims of appreciation — or how much should our doubts concern us?

RESPONDING TO "GLOW" AND "SCHMOOZE"

When students have a less-than-sophisticated sense of the rhetorical situation, or a limited understanding of self-assessment, they may rely on "schmoozing," and instructors need to prepare themselves for the "schmooze factor" when grading portfolios. Weiser calls it "psyching out the port. prof," sometimes in the form of "writing to warm the heart of a composition teacher" (1997, 300). This may be in the form of praising our teaching — "You're the best teacher I've ever had" — or making grand claims for their improvement in writing — "My writing has improved more in one semester than it did in four years of high school." Students know what we want to hear and can sometimes put together a portfolio that "glows" in the beginning but isn't particularly strong or consistent after the glowing introduction. Evaluators of classroom portfolios need to be aware of these phenomena and to pay attention to their own readings of students' reflective pieces and what they find themselves responding to or valuing.

First, it may be difficult to distinguish schmooze from sincerity, but I want to suggest that students who express gratitude or who praise our abilities as teachers may not be intentionally schmoozing but may be trying to show that they are targeting a particular audience and understand what that audience values. They also may be sincere. We are often in a position of judging someone's sincerity (politicians come to mind, or deans and provosts), and we have to make the call based on past experience, intuition, evidence, or whatever data we can collect. The same goes for judging our students' sincerity or credibility in their portfolio's reflective introductions or cover letters: We have to rely on our own judgment.

One way to resist the schmooze factor is not to give students models of reflective introductions that contain any passages that could be interpreted as schmoozing. If students think you value praise of your teaching or appeals to how much they've learned, they will, naturally, use that as one of their own appeals. Another (rather authoritarian) way to prevent schmoozing is simply to outlaw it.

It is also an option to ask for the portfolios with names and identifiable features removed: to judge and record grades using social security numbers, for example. While this anonymity might reduce the feeling of pride and ownership that portfolios help to build in students, it should reduce any anxiety teachers have about judging degrees of schmooze.

Judging Degrees of Schmooze

Are the following excerpts from reflective introductions examples of schmoozing? How can we tell? Aren't we more likely to call it schmoozing if it comes from a student who has done mediocre work, with only a modicum of effort? Or from a student whose skills are not that strong, someone who may be facing an average grade? Or a student we just don't like very much, with whom we've had a personality conflict?

One fuzzy category, within the area of schmoozing, is what I call *transformation narratives*. These are fairly common moves in reflective introductions, when students claim that the course somehow changed them or truly affected them. (See in particular Kristin's opening line on page 52.)

When I walked into this class for the first time in September, I had no idea what I was capable of in writing. I had no idea what I could or could not do. I had never written to an audience before. I had only written to one specific person, the teacher. This class showed me what it was like to write to an audience, both specific and general, and to change my writing accordingly. Also, all I had ever done were reports and critiques, no open letters, commentaries, or proposals. I wasn't fully aware of the different types of writing I had to choose from. This class made me realize that there are many different styles and genres of writing. — *Carol*

> I had never expressed myself artistically or intellectually as a writer and came to this course relatively new to writing. I say that now, for it wasn't until I attempted to write that I realized how little I knew. Writing requires a great deal of contemplation, clarity of mind, perseverance and time. I have gained a new respect for those who choose this medium. It has been interesting for me to join their world and enter this realm. — *Karen*

When students rely on stock narratives provided by the culture — "This experience has changed me in profound ways" — it's difficult to fault them. They have found and used, after all, a culturally sanctioned form in which to express their experience.

If passages like the following appear in portfolio introductions of the best students, are we as likely to consider it schmoozing? Consider the following:

> I liked this class. It allowed me to write about what I was thinking — unlike previous classes in which I was forced to write about a boring topic not even of my choice. This class has given me the chance to express my ideas and opinions, and I liked that. — *Joel*

> In my personal life there is a letter that I need to write that I have been putting off. Through your class I have learned how to think it out, write it, and rework it so that I can present the best final product possible. I think the valuable skills that I've learned this semester will improve my writing as I continue my education and will enhance my personal writing as well. Thank you for removing the sinking feeling of dread that once came over me when the idea of writing was proposed. — *Amy*

> In conclusion, I would like to say that I enjoyed this class because I was able to improve my writing through the course, and I think that this portfolio demonstrates that well. Happy reading! — *Kristin*

In a less predictable way, some students will touch on the standard narrative, and then give it a refreshing twist:

> I must admit, upon hearing this course description, my heart sank a little. I had never dedicated any time to travel writing. In fact, the thought of spending an entire semester focused on it made me contemplate dropping the course. After looking over the syllabus and sitting through the first class, I decided to try it. I thought maybe I was being a tad close-minded about the topic and perhaps I would end up falling in love with the whole thing. I am still not too crazy about travel writing. I can honestly say that I will not be making an appearance on the <u>New York Times</u> best sellers' list within the genre of travel writing. However, I did learn quite a bit this semester and am anxious to share some work with you. — *Karina*

Whether we "trust" the writer or the writer's claims is a valid way of responding to a text. Schmoozing can fall, after all, within the category of the ethical appeal, or the appeal from character. What kind of character comes through in the prose? I tend to trust writers more who thank their peer group members rather than thanking me, or those who refer to specific activities or goals of the class, rather than to the course more generally. "I learned a lot in this class" isn't persuasive, but this might be: "I learned a lot from choosing my own topics, doing the postwrites, and reading your comments on my drafts." If this sentence were followed by an illustrative "For example," I would be very convinced by that writer's claim. "My writing really improved" is not as convincing as "I have learned to distinguish facts from claims, anecdotes from arguments, and support from repetition." So, as I tell my students, specificity is almost always better than vagueness in these situations. As with any strong piece of writing, reflective essays should contain details, evidence, support, or examples from the student's writing.

Portfolios that glow in the beginning and then grow dim should be evaluated as a package. Tempting as it is to reward writers who are comfortable with self-reflection or with the identity of "writer" (see Black, et al. 1994), if the portfolio does not meet the expectations set by the successful introduction, then the assessment will have to account for the lapse in quality.

Anticipating elements of glow and schmooze does not mean that we become suspicious of students who claim in their reflective introductions to have learned a great deal, grown as writers, or enjoyed our class. It does mean recognizing that writers call on a number of strategies for being reflective learners, and some will be more effective than others with us as readers.

—10—
Managing the Paper Load and Other Concerns

A writing program director said to me recently, "Oh, we'd like to use portfolios, but I can't possibly ask the graduate teaching assistants to do all that grading at the end of the semester when they are also writing papers for the courses they're taking." Because so many writing programs rely on contingent faculty — graduate teaching assistants also completing coursework and part-time or adjunct faculty who may also teach at other institutions — the end-of-term responsibility of portfolio teaching does become a significant issue. How can graduate teaching assistants and overworked contingent faculty feel comfortable with evaluating portfolios at the end of a term?

Portfolios do not create "more" grading and need not add more work to the busiest time of a term. Portfolio teaching shifts the assessment from summative to formative, and keeps it there for as long as possible. In fact, by removing the pressure of putting grades on every draft, teachers benefit in several ways. For new teachers using portfolios, "they have time to gain confidence in their ability to evaluate writing. They do not have to assign a grade to a paper after they have only been teaching a few weeks; they have time to learn to evaluate before they assign grades" (Weiser 1997, 298). Teachers, experienced or not, also benefit from not having to return papers with poor grades. First-year students, often having relied on a one-shot draft method throughout high school, can be shocked by "college" grades or may be unprepared for the more rigorous expectations of college writing. Returning papers with C's, D's, and F's was the worst experience of my early teaching career. I learned quickly not to return graded essays at the beginning of class because students would become sullen and withdrawn or preoccupied and anxious, killing any class discussion or participation. So I'd wait until near the end of a class to return them, but my sense of dread never decreased. Giving new teachers a break from this situation increases the chances that their classes will go more smoothly, without angry students challenging their authority or without their spending eleven hours on twenty-two papers.

Finally, reading and grading portfolios takes no more time at the end of the semester than does reading and grading any set of final essays. In fact, it might even take less time, for me, because I make minimal comments. Without writing the end comment or the long note that begins "If you revise," the grading time is cut by at least half. There is "more" to read, yes. Portfolios often consist of three or four essays or their equivalent; however, without making corrections, writing marginal or end comments, or "justify-ing" the grade, reading a portfolio of twenty pages takes no more time than responding to a final paper of five pages.

As one fairly new writing teacher related to me recently, she found that portfolios probably would have saved her time in the long run. Caught in a classic bind of process writing classes, she allowed endless revisions of papers — to improve the grade — and lived to regret it. Because she knows the value of revision and could not resist allowing students to revise, this instructor granted revisions for any student who wished to improve his or her grade on a returned paper. In other words, she papered herself into a grading corner. If most students take a teacher up on her offer that they may "revise to improve their grade," then well-meaning instructors will confront at least three related problems: (1) creating more paper reading than they would have to do with a structured portfolio method, (2) making sometimes torturous decisions about whether the revision has definitely improved the paper from a C+ to a B-, and (3) sending students the wrong message that *any* changes will mean improvement, or that revision always results in a measurably "bet-ter" paper. The portfolio rewards students for effort without continually putting the teacher in the position of "grader." In addition, a portfolio method requires less grading overall.

Let's say you have 100 students in a given semester, and each writes five papers. Peer response groups read the first or discovery draft, and you read and respond to the next version, for a total of 500 responses. If you put grades on each of these and allow any of these 500 papers to be revised to improve the grade, you could potentially be reading 500 again, for a total of 1,000. But if you ask students to submit a portfolio of their three best works, that's a mere 300 additional readings! The key difference, however, is that in each of the two rounds of traditional grading — assigning a letter grade to each essay — instructors would have to weigh, consider, rank, judge, and decide on 1,000 individual grades, with the added pressure, in round two, of whether the paper is truly better. With the portfolio method, you decide on a grade for the entire package, which saves hours of weighing, considering, ranking, sorting, judg-ing, and *worrying*.

Of course, there will be exceptions to this neat equation: With an open revision policy, not all students will submit revisions, and certainly with a portfolio method, some students will ask you to read their revised versions a second or third time before they submit them in the portfolio. In addition, if teachers choose to evaluate the working folder, there is that round of grading as well. I am convinced, however, that portfolios reduce the total amount of time spent grading papers while increasing the quality and meaningfulness of the assessment situation.

OTHER SPECIAL CONCERNS

What if students decide very early in the process that they just won't pursue an essay to the portfolio stage? If not every essay or project "gets a grade," isn't this a loophole that many students will find immediately?

Teachers with years of experience as motivators will see this potential problem: If individual papers are not graded, then where's the student's motivation for completing the assignment? If students only need, say, three out of five of the assigned essays in the portfolio, why should they write the other two? This is something teachers should consider, but I want to resist making pedagogical decisions around potentially lazy students.

You can't "make" students write every assignment if they figure out ways to cut corners. Policing them is not our job. Here are the ways, however, in which lazy students will be penalized in my classes if they think they've found a loophole or decide to "blow off" an assignment. First, if students come to class on workshop day (for peer response group meetings) without a full working draft, I record an unexcused absence. They are welcome to stay to be a reader, but they are counted absent (and unexcused absences add up to penalties, of course). Second, students must do a postwrite for each essay that they turn in for my response; without a postwrite, I won't read the draft, and they lose five possible points. Third, students will be penalized for an incomplete or thin working folder. Finally, in a less tangible way, students who don't do an assignment will have fewer choices to make for the portfolio, making the papers they did write count *more* or have a more critical outcome. If students have not been through a full, recursive process on all five projects, their portfolio introductions or reflective essays will show that lapse: Students who have not done the work cannot be very convincing about what they've learned.

A well-designed portfolio class is not an invitation to laziness — far from it. Indeed, because of the emphasis on revision — the portfolio method insists that students learn to revise and edit — portfolio courses are more rigorous than more traditional courses in which every paper is graded after the second or third draft.

Another special concern: What do you do with the "good student" who has "nothing to do" the last three weeks? This question was posed to me by a group of English teachers at community colleges in Connecticut, where I was giving a presentation on portfolio teaching. This problem may emerge when teachers have a wide range of abilities in a composition class, as many of us do. In our efforts near the end of a semester to make sure that some students turn in passing work, we really shouldn't neglect the students whose work shines. They can be working toward improvement as well. Confident, bright students who write well can be paired or grouped together for the last two or three weeks of the course, forming their own workshop group to guide one another's revisions, and teachers might be able to meet with this group at least once to discuss their choices and to work on expanding or polishing their papers. Writing centers may be able to help these students, too, by giving them an opportunity to share their work with a trained tutor. Perhaps the best way to give good writers some attention on their portfolio production, however, is to design opportunities for them to share their work with a wider audience, as the next chapter discusses.

—11—
Sharing or Publishing Portfolios

All students, but particularly those who excel at writing, can benefit from sharing, publishing, or disseminating their portfolio to a wider audience than the immediate writing class. When compiling, organizing, and polishing their portfolios, writers might want the opportunity to share the products of their labor with others. Such opportunities support the rhetorical emphasis of the course and encourage students to produce "presentation-quality" portfolios. The literature on portfolios emphasizes the importance of using them not just internally to establish a course grade but also externally to heighten students' sense of audience and purpose. This recognition of a portfolio's powerful reach beyond school writing has led to a number of adaptations or discussions of electronic portfolios (Hawisher and Selfe 1997; Wickliff 1997; Fischer 1997; Blair and Takayoshi 1997).

Many students need to be coaxed out of writing only for the teacher, and sharing drafts routinely, through peer response groups and other methods, can accomplish this. While they may be writing to a specific audience suited to their purpose — environmentalists, construction workers, or soccer fans — students can also benefit from the awareness that "anyone" might read this — unknown readers who might be browsing the Web, for example. Electronic portfolios, especially those in hypertext, demand that students have good reasons for hot links or buttons, and ask them to consider how they want readers to move through a site.

Donna Reiss at Tidewater Community College (TCC) has developed a Webfolio program that was "designed to be a dynamic electronic record of student activities at the college. The individual class pages are designed as reflective portfolios that both illustrate student work and also provide a culminating work integrating course content and concepts" (Reiss). Using a template, writers post assignments to their Web page that meet with the instructor's criteria and fulfill the expectations that other readers at TCC — and beyond — may have.

Having your own students post portfolios to a Web page is not difficult, although it will take some time and a bit of technical know-how. Your students can use an FTP program to upload files from their computer's hard drive to your school's network server. (FTP, or File Transfer Protocol, is a set of guidelines that lets you transfer files between different computers on the Internet.) Windows users have many FTP programs to choose from (such as CuteFTP and WSFTP_32), and some of them are available as freeware. The most popular FTP program for Macintosh users is Fetch. It is free to those affiliated with an educational institution. Your school's computer lab will most likely have FTP software already installed. If not, you can use a search engine (such as Google.com or Metacrawler.com) to find FTP programs on the Web.

Technology is not, however, the only way to share portfolios or to celebrate the culmination of a semester's work. Some low-tech ways to achieve the same ends (a heightened awareness of audience, for example) include the following:

- Put course portfolios on reserve in the library, to remain there through the next semester or for the year.
- Have a poster session or portfolio fair in a large public space where students can display their portfolios and talk with other writers.
- Ask students to read aloud in class.
- Exchange portfolios with other classes.
- Put two classes together and have a reading session.

Teachers will find other simple ways of sharing portfolios, depending on their situations and purposes. One writing program administrator I know, for example, keeps teaching assistant portfolios in her office, available to other TAs through an on-your-honor sign-out basis. Teaching assistants are encouraged to look at one another's portfolios to get ideas for their own and to feel connected to a teaching community. Finding ways to keep portfolios in order to share them as models might address some of the practical concerns of portfolio teaching — that is, What do we do with all of the (paper) folders when the course is over? If you can't return each portfolio to its writer before the term ends, then ask students to submit a stamped, self-addressed manila envelope, so you can mail them their portfolios after grades are due. Or let students know how they can retrieve their portfolios the following semester. Unreturned or unclaimed portfolios can be kept for a year or two, depending on space, and then discarded. For adjuncts or teaching assistants without office storage space, the writing program director should arrange to keep portfolios for a stated period of time. Portfolios sitting in storage, however, are not serving a useful purpose; ideally, students will reclaim them or upload them onto the Web, or instructors will save them and, with permission, use them as models or to inform a teacher-research project.

As they should, teachers will create their own ways to encourage the sharing of portfolios or to extend the portfolio's reach beyond the classroom walls. As with all of the options inherent in the portfolio principles of choice, variety, and reflection, sharing the results can take many forms but supports the rhetorical nature of the portfolio process as well as the importance of a final product. Portfolios are an adaptable, flexible teaching tool on which many writing teachers depend. I hope that this teaching guide has given you some ideas for incorporating portfolios into your own teaching contexts or writing programs.

An Annotated Bibliography on Teacher-Graded Classroom Portfolios

The literature on portfolios is vast. From kindergarten to college and from math to writing, from classroom learning portfolios to statewide competency assessments, the coverage on portfolios continues to increase as educators find new uses for them. In keeping with the focus of *Portfolio Teaching*, here are annotations for a selected number of resources that address portfolios in college (and secondary) writing classrooms. There are a large number of good articles on administering large-scale portfolio assessments or portfolio writing programs; however, I have limited this bibliography to portfolios for classrooms. My purpose is simply to share what I have found most helpful in my efforts to develop portfolio practices and an understanding of assessment and reflection that my students can take with them into other contexts.

Belanoff, Pat, and Marcia Dickson, eds. *Portfolios: Process and Product.* Portsmouth, NH: Heinemann, 1991.
    The first portfolio book in my library, this volume inaugurated a decade of research on and growing interest in portfolios. This collection opens with two essays by Pat Belanoff and Peter Elbow on the portfolio program at the State University of New York at Stony Brook. The second one, "Using Portfolios to Increase Collaboration and Community in a Writing Program," was one of the first journal articles to stimulate interest in writing portfolios at the college level (*Writing Program Administration* 9.3 [1986]: 27–40). Of the twenty-three essays, many are devoted to proficiency testing, program assessment, and political issues, but seven are specifically related to the classroom. Jeffrey Sommers's essay advocates portfolios for the ways in which they bring response practices in line with composing process theories. He describes two portfolio models, one a portfolio grading system and the other a holistic portfolio system, each of which addresses issues of response in theoretically different ways. Kathy McClelland emphasizes the importance of self-evaluation and of postponing grades until the end of the course, both of which are crucial elements to classroom portfolios. Kerry Weinbaum calls reflective self-assessment letters the most important aspect of the portfolio process, and describes her use of a contract system to personalize the portfolio system for students. In addition, Bonnie Hain's essay helped me to make a case for offering a portfolio option in our M.A. program, and Cherryl Armstrong Smith has a very thoughtful essay on "Writing without Testing."

Black, Laurel, et al., eds. *New Directions in Portfolio Assessment: Reflective Practice, Critical Theory, and Large-Scale Scoring.* Portsmouth, NH: Boynton/Cook, 1994.
    This collection resulted from a 1992 conference of the same name at Miami University, one of the first national conferences dedicated to portfolio assessment. The

twenty-six essays include several on portfolios for writing programs or large-scale assessments, while others have implications for teacher-graded classroom portfolios. Several different kinds of classrooms are covered: fiction writing classes (Tom Romano), science writing classes (John Beall), K–12 classes (Sandra Murphy), and graduate classes (Nedra Reynolds). Chris Anson argues for the value of teaching portfolios when they are an integral part of the writing program. Kathleen Blake Yancey outlines the time, resources, and guidance that new teachers need before they begin to use portfolios, and Irwin Weiser details the benefits, for both students and new teachers of writing, of portfolio evaluation. Glenda Conway's essay on portfolio cover letters has been extremely helpful in my own attempt to study reflective introductions. In addition, for issues related to reading and grading portfolios, essays by Laurel Black et al. and Gail Stygall et al. are fascinating accounts of the ways in which our readings assign gender to students.

> Black, Laurel, et al. "Writing like a Woman and Being Rewarded for It: Gender, Assessment, and Reflective Letters from Miami University Student Portfolios." *New Directions in Portfolio Assessment: Reflective Practice, Critical Theory, and Large-Scale Scoring.* Ed. Laurel Black, Donald A. Daiker, Jeffrey Sommers, and Gail Stygall. Portsmouth, NH: Boynton/Cook, 1994. 235–47.

In one of the most interesting research studies of portfolios, Black and her co-authors, once alerted to the fact that females were faring better than males in Miami University's portfolio placement program, analyzed the reflective letters of a representative sampling of portfolios. They found a number of differences consistent with the findings of other researchers; most significantly, female writers "position themselves in relation to others" (239). Women were more likely to depict themselves as writers in these letters and to establish a closer relationship with the reader, while men were more likely to identify with the institution and the assessment situation. This study alerted me to the importance of paying attention to my own reflective letter assignment: Was I encouraging students to take risks in these introductions that might advantage women writers (246)? The reflective introduction need not be a confessional piece, and students should have enough options within that important assignment to write successfully, even if they don't write "personally."

> Conway, Glenda. "Portfolio Cover Letters, Students' Self-Presentation, and Teachers' Ethics." *New Directions in Portfolio Assessment: Reflective Practice, Critical Theory, and Large-Scale Scoring.* Ed. Laurel Black, Donald A. Daiker, Jeffrey Sommers, and Gail Stygall. Portsmouth, NH: Boynton/Cook, 1994. 83–92.

Beginning with the safe assumption that cover letters are the most consistently required document in portfolios, Conway reminds us of their rhetorical importance as the first piece in the portfolio, the one "that gets to speak the portfolio's first words" (84). With the power to engage or alienate an audience, cover letters need more of our attention, especially when they may determine how we evaluate a portfolio. Conway emphatically recommends that the cover letter not be students' first or only attempt at reflection.

Gill, Kent, ed., and the Committee on Classroom Practices. *Process and Portfolios in Writing Instruction*. Urbana, IL: NCTE, 1993.

The first section of this collection covers various strategies in the process writing classroom — scavenger hunts, life maps, and glossing, for example — but the second section is devoted to "Exploiting the Portfolio," credited here for honoring writing, motivating revision, and developing student sensitivity to good writing. Many of the contributing authors in these chapters are affiliated with the Northern Virginia Writing Project. Bob Ingalls's essay on "Interviewing a Portfolio" introduces a clever way of introducing rubrics to students, and Donald Gallehr outlines the schedule and expectations that he has developed for portfolio assessment. Laura Brady and Christopher Thaiss explain the evolution of a portfolio proficiency assessment for juniors and seniors, including a timed process essay and assessment by the major department. Brady and Thaiss model the type of reflection — what they've learned from the whole experience — that portfolio practitioners begin to develop and value.

Graves, Donald H., and Bonnie Sunstein, eds. *Portfolio Portraits*. Portsmouth, NH: Heinemann, 1992.

As most edited collections on portfolios do, this volume includes essays on portfolios from the perspectives of classroom use and large-scale assessment, but it also offers four portraits of portfolio keepers — a superintendent, a college senior, and two children, one a bilingual learner. In addition, several different kinds of writers are profiled in the section on classroom practice: first, fifth, and eighth graders; college sophomores; and teachers. For my purposes, Elizabeth Chiseri-Strater's essay, "College Sophomores Reopen the Closed Portfolio," is most useful because she reflects on her own movement from writing folders — a physical receptacle for holding students' written work — to open portfolios, where students have the responsibility for assigning a certain weight to each portfolio paper.

Hamp-Lyons, Liz, and William Condon. "Questioning Assumptions about Portfolio-Based Assessment." *College Composition and Communication* 44.2 (May 1993): 176–90.

In an attempt to establish criteria and build consensus during portfolio assessment, these researchers developed a reading log activity for portfolio readers. The collected data revealed "imponderables in the human dimensions of portfolio assessment" (178) and challenged five key assumptions held by many portfolio teachers. They conclude that the benefits of portfolio assessment to a writing program faculty are sizable — including better communication — but some of their findings do have implications for classroom portfolio systems; for example, that students may be ill-advised to "save the best for last"; that readers may not attend equally to the entire portfolio; and that readers often arrive at a score during the reading of the first paper (182). These findings have influenced my own advice and guidance to students, but I am left unconvinced that students should be encouraged, even required, to include drafts in their portfolios (185). While expanding the portfolio to include drafts or process evidence may be appropriate in a local context, such as Michigan's English Composition Board, I believe it is appropriate, for my own classroom portfolios, to emphasize a final product as a culmination of the process.

Herter, Roberta J. "Writing Portfolios: Alternatives to Testing." *English Journal* 80.1 (Jan. 1991): 90–91.

Herter illustrates how portfolios connect to and shape classroom practice, and how they can affect other areas of instruction. Portfolios become richer and fuller, for example, when teachers trust students to generate their own topics. Students found more reasons to collaborate and began to develop criteria for measuring the success of writing in different genres. Students' responsibility figures large in this account of classroom portfolio assessment.

Journal of Teaching Writing. Indiana Teachers of Writing. Special Issue on Portfolios, 12.1 (1992).

This issue of *JTW* includes eight articles on a range of issues related to portfolios but all concerned with the integrity of a portfolio method. Douglas Hesse questions how to define "variety" in portfolios, especially considering the divide between academic and personal writing, and he argues for the role of public discourse in students' portfolios. Mary Lynch Kennedy warns against a "backward" development, whereby portfolios are embraced before they are examined, and she describes a method for using portfolios to conduct a review of the writing program and to build interpretive communities. One article tracks new teachers as they begin to incorporate portfolios, concluding that they could not simply insert portfolios in an old curriculum (Bishop and Crossley), and another describes the use of portfolios to design teacher evaluations (Hult). Richard Bullock's review of four books on portfolios, all published in 1991 or 1992, concludes this issue, and he praises the Graves and Sunstein book as having the best approach to keeping teachers invested in portfolios.

Paulson, F. Leon, Pearl R. Paulson, and Carol A. Meyer. "What Makes a Portfolio a Portfolio?" *Educational Leadership* Feb. 1991: 60–63.

This article offers a very useful definition of portfolios, one that emphasizes variety, student choice, and self-reflection. Focusing on the ways that instruction and assessment can be woven together through portfolios, the authors offer eight guidelines — for example, that a portfolio is different from a cumulative folder and that a portfolio may serve a different purpose during the year from the purpose it serves at the end. These authors do recommend the use of models, so that students can see how others develop and reflect on portfolios.

Wolf, Kenneth P. "The Schoolteacher's Portfolio: Practical Issues in Design, Implementation, and Evaluation." *Phi Delta Kappan* Oct. 1991: 129–36.

Wolf shares the design and results of a four-year study of teacher evaluation at Stanford University. Portfolios, according to Wolf, "hold great promise for teacher evaluation but are fraught with potential problems." Some of the practical problems are that portfolios are "messy to construct, cumbersome to store, and costly to evaluate." More significantly, if evaluated in a perfunctory fashion, portfolios can become an obstacle to good teaching. Portfolios can, however, serve a formative function for teachers and can capture the complexities of teaching.

Yancey, Kathleen Blake, ed. *Portfolios in the Writing Classroom: An Introduction.* Urbana, IL: NCTE, 1992.

This is the second portfolio book on my shelves, preceded only by Belanoff and Dickson. With consistent quality, these ten essays focus on the changes that portfolios bring to the writing classroom — showing how, for example, they increase student autonomy (Sue Ellen Gold) and contribute to "ecological evaluation" (Catharine Lucas) or authentic assessment. Catherine D'Aoust offers a very practical guide to a portfolio's purposes, including such details as housing and managing them. Roberta Camp discusses the role of reflection — the importance of introducing it early, for example — as well as the writing inventory and portfolio updates. Several of the contributors to this practical, useful collection have gone on to become portfolio experts: Sandra Murphy, Mary Ann Smith, Irwin Weiser, and Kathleen Blake Yancey.

Yancey, Kathleen Blake, and Irwin Weiser, eds. *Situating Portfolios: Four Perspectives.* Logan, UT: Utah State UP, 1997.

This is the most recent anthology, one that reflects the growing sophistication of portfolio theories and approaches. In addition to chapters on portfolios in doctoral programs (Heiges) and in law school (Dailey), five essays in the technology section address hypertext authoring, hypertext portfolios, electronic portfolios, and assessing portfolios over "Portnet." The best of these for those just beginning to try electronic portfolios are the chapters by Kristine Blair and Pamela Takayoshi and by Gail Hawisher and Cynthia Selfe. Targeted to college instructors, this collection's strongest section — again, for my purposes — is on teaching and professional development, where the editors contribute their own essays on teacher portfolios in methods courses, and where the other three excellent chapters, while focused on teacher portfolios, offer many implications and ideas for any college classroom portfolio situation. Peter Elbow and Pat Belanoff open this volume with "Reflections on an Explosion," and there are a few selections on large-scale assessment. In the pedagogy section, however, readers will appreciate Mary Ann Smith's chapter, "Behind the Scenes: Portfolios in a Classroom Learning Community," in which she recommends the "living arrangements" that accommodate portfolios best; she profiles several different classroom learning communities. Mary Perry, in "Producing Purposeful Portfolios," discusses her students' design of different scoring rubrics — one for college admissions and one for employment — to guide their selections of their portfolio's contents.

Works Cited

Anson, Chris M. "Portfolios for Teachers: Writing Our Way to Reflective Practice." Black, Daiker, Sommers, and Stygall 185–200.

Atwell, Nancie. *In the Middle: New Understandings about Writing, Reading, and Learning.* 2nd ed. Portsmouth, NH: Boynton/Cook, 1998.

Black, Laurel, Donald A. Daiker, Jeffrey Sommers, and Gail Stygall, eds. *New Directions in Portfolio Assessment: Reflective Practice, Critical Theory, and Large-Scale Scoring.* Portsmouth, NH: Boynton/Cook, 1994.

Black, Laurel, et al. "Writing like a Woman and Being Rewarded for It: Gender, Assessment, and Reflective Letters from Miami University Student Portfolios." Black, Daiker, Sommers, and Stygall 235–47.

Blair, Kristine L., and Pamela Takayoshi. "Reflections in Reading and Evaluating Electronic Portfolios." Yancey and Weiser 357–69.

Burch, C. Beth. "Finding Out What's in Their Heads: Using Teacher Portfolios to Assess English Education Students — and Programs." Yancey and Weiser 263–77.

Conway, Glenda. "Portfolio Cover Letters, Students' Self-Presentation, and Teachers' Ethics." Black, Daiker, Sommers, and Stygall 83–92.

Corbett, Edward P. J., and Robert J. Connors. *Classical Rhetoric for the Modern Student.* 4th ed. New York: Oxford UP, 1999.

Daiker, Donald A., and Max Morenberg, eds. *The Writing Teacher as Researcher: Essays in the Theory and Practice of Class-Based Research.* Portsmouth, NH: Boynton/Cook, 1990.

Elbow, Peter, and Pat Belanoff. "Reflections on an Explosion: Portfolios in the '90s and Beyond." Yancey and Weiser 21–33.

Fischer, Katherine M. "Down the Yellow Chip Road: Hypertext Portfolios in Oz." Yancey and Weiser 338–56.

Gaughn, John. *Cultural Reflections: Critical Teaching and Learning in the English Classroom.* Portsmouth, NH: Boynton/Cook, 1997.

Hamp-Lyons, Liz, and William Condon. "Questioning Assumptions about Portfolio-Based Assessment." *College Composition and Communication* 44.2 (May 1993): 176–90.

Hawisher, Gail E., and Cynthia L. Selfe. "Wedding the Technologies of Writing Portfolios and Computers: The Challenges of Electronic Classrooms." Yancey and Weiser 305–21.

hooks, bell. *Teaching to Transgress: Education as the Practice of Freedom.* New York: Routledge, 1994.

Lindemann, Erika. *A Rhetoric for Writing Teachers.* 3rd ed. New York: Oxford UP, 1995.

Murray, Donald. *A Writer Teaches Writing: A Practical Method of Teaching Composition.* Boston: Houghton Mifflin, 1968.

"Our Beliefs about Portfolios." *The Council Chronicle* (June 1997): 11.

Ray, Ruth E. *The Practice of Theory: Teacher Research in Composition.* Urbana, IL: NCTE, 1993.

Reiss, Donna. "Student Webfolio Project Introduction: Tidewater Community College." 18 Apr. 1999 <http://www.tc.va.us/faculty/tcreisd/resource/webfolio/>.

Rich, Adrienne. "Teaching Language in Open Admissions." *On Lies, Secrets, and Silence: Selected Prose, 1966–78.* New York: Norton, 1979.

Smith, Summer. "The Genre of the End Comment: Conventions in Teacher Responses to Student Writing." *College Composition and Communication* 48.2 (May 1997): 249–68.

Sommers, Jeffrey. "The Writer's Memo: Collaboration, Response, and Development." *Writing and Response: Theory, Practice, Research.* Ed. Chris M. Anson. Urbana, IL: NCTE, 1989.

Straub, Richard. "The Concept of Control in Teacher Response: Defining the Varieties of 'Directive' and 'Facilitative' Commentary." *College Composition and Communication* 47.2 (May 1996): 223–51.

Weiser, Irwin. "Revising Our Practices: How Portfolios Help Teachers Learn." Yancey and Weiser 293–301.

Wickliff, Gregory A. "A Hypertext Authoring Course, Portfolio Assessment, and Diversity." Yancey and Weiser 322–37.

Yagelski, Robert P. "Portfolios as a Way to Encourage Reflective Practice among Preservice English Teachers." Yancey and Weiser 225–43.

Yancey, Kathleen Blake. *Reflection in the Writing Classroom.* Logan, UT: Utah State UP, 1998.

———. "Teacher Portfolios: Lessons in Resistance, Readiness, and Reflection." Yancey and Weiser 244–62.

Yancey, Kathleen Blake, and Irwin Weiser, eds. *Situating Portfolios.* Logan, UT: Utah UP, 1997.